DOLBEN LIBRARY

Northfield Mount Hermon School
Northfield, Massachusetts

◆

ROBERT KENNEDY

THE LAST CAMPAIGN

ROBERT KENNEDY
THE LAST CAMPAIGN

Photographs by BILL EPPRIDGE
Text by HAYS GOREY

With a Foreword by
PRESIDENT BILL CLINTON

Harcourt Brace & Company
NEW YORK   SAN DIEGO   LONDON

D

Staff photographs by William Eppridge, used by permission of *Life* magazine
and Time, Inc.

Library of Congress Catalog Card Number 93-12572

ISBN 0-15-178320-9

Printed in the United States of America

First edition

A B C D E

A note about the photographs:

The photographs in this book were taken by Bill Eppridge, on
assignment for *Life*. They record Robert F. Kennedy's political
activities as a New York senator in 1966 — especially his
campaigning in support of Democratic candidates across the
country — and they document his 1968 campaign seeking the
Democratic nomination to the presidency.

Picture Editor: Adrienne Aurichio
Designed by: Lydia D'moch
Design concept: Bill Eppridge and Adrienne Aurichio

These photographs are dedicated to my family, Theresa and Edward Eppridge, Terry Eppridge, Randi and Roger Norum and their children, Tracy and Roger, who shared with me the exhilaration and then the final nightmare of this campaign and endured with me the subsequent years of anguished recollections. Perhaps now, with the publication of these pictures, a spirit is freed.

B. E.

To Brooke, Erinn, Nonie, Matt, Shannon
And to Betsy, Kerry, Lara, Daniel, Anne

Let us contemplate our forefathers, and posterity,
and resolve to maintain the rights bequeathed to us
from the former, for the sake of the later.
— *Samuel Adams*

H. G.

FOREWORD

A couple of days before our graduation from college, my roommates and I went to sleep full of hope — then woke to despair. Seconds after Robert F. Kennedy declared victory in the California Democratic primary, we switched off the television, not knowing until morning that he, too, had been felled by a bullet.

From that bleak Wednesday's dawn, through all the years that followed, it often seemed that his assassin had taken aim at and struck not merely a man — the last of three heroes — but our country's very sense of its own possibilities and finest nature.

This superb volume of prose and photographs summons the remarkable life of Robert Kennedy to the forefront of our memories; it makes us feel again his force as the distinctive public servant of his day.

Robert Kennedy was a statesman who loved politics and yet whose contributions were uncharacteristic of that arena. At a time when citizens felt disconnected from their leaders, he had an uncommon feel for what people experienced in their lives. He spoke new truths to audiences benumbed by the expedient glibness of conventional politicians.

He fought to close the chasm between working-class whites and blacks while others sought political advantage in prying them apart. He was skeptical about bureaucracies and programs — as if either could solve our problems without private and individual efforts. He spoke plainly and passionately about hunger, about the unequal distribution of wealth and power in America, about ending apartheid in South Africa, and about the glories of citizens taking responsibility for their own actions and their own behavior.

The hardest edges of his dissent were burnished by even deeper expressions of patriotism. He was a singularly unifying figure, especially appreciated by those of us who stood in opposition to America's role in Vietnam. For he reminded supporters of the war that men and women could bear faithful allegiance to our country — and love it with all their hearts — even as they strongly disagreed with its leaders' policies.

That is why, as we recall his loss a quarter century ago, we must dedicate ourselves anew to his example. After all the lies and disappointments, the shredded promises and documents, the gridlock and the deadlock that have paralyzed the democratic system he so loved, what remains at the heart of our experience is the hope he embodied: that Americans, as Robert Kennedy said, "can do bettah." And when we try, we always do.

Hays Gorey's words and Bill Eppridge's pictures both serve as inspiration and pay tribute to Robert Kennedy's heroic journey, his rare blend of moral courage and intellectual openness, his steadfast faith in first principles, and his readiness to rise to the unpredictable occasion.

BILL CLINTON
President of the United States
April 1993

Despite a wait of two and a half hours for Bobby to appear at this 1966 rally in Sioux City, Iowa, the crowd's attention has not waned.

THE LAUNCH

"I Cannot Stand Aside"

It was 1968, and an earthquake had shaken the political landscape. Robert Kennedy, the brother of a legend and himself already an idol, had ended months of personal agonizing in March by declaring himself a candidate for the presidential nomination of the Democratic party. An unhappy nation, at war in Vietnam and bitterly divided over the justice of that war, had been faced with what to millions was a dismal choice for president: the incumbent, Lyndon Johnson, or the former vice president, Richard Nixon. Neither one excited the electorate, nor did either appear to comprehend the magnitude or the crippling effect of the national division over Vietnam. Yet it seemed inevitable that one or the other would be elected president in November. The unwinnable war would continue, rioters would torch the cities, and despair would tighten its grip on America. A brave opponent of the war, Senator

Eugene McCarthy, had already challenged the incumbent president, but few thought that McCarthy could make it to the top. Robert Kennedy just might.

Suddenly there was hope for some; for others, dread. Robert Kennedy, about whom few Americans were neutral, represented courage and truth to his admirers and epitomized ruthlessness and arrogance to his plentiful detractors. He would defy convention, risking his political future at the age of forty-two by challenging the man who had been John Kennedy's vice president, Lyndon Johnson. Whatever the outcome, the campaign year of 1968 would be transformed from crashing bore to gripping drama. The opposition to the war would, at long last, have a voice — thin and reedy at times, but one that would nonetheless be heard in the rough-and-tumble of national politics.

America was about to experience a candidate for president who would not pander, dissemble, or sugarcoat, one who would be accessible — signing autographs, answering voters' questions, and even telling them off — someone they could walk up to and touch, without interference from the Secret Service. There was another, more substantive aspect that would make this campaign the last of its kind: those who cheered his entry did so because they knew that he would, if elected, try to do what he had said he would do. Those who opposed his candidacy did so because they knew that, too.

History has no parallel to Robert Kennedy. In 1968, he was a very junior United States senator from New York, and yet he was as well known nationally and internationally as Lyndon Johnson, the Texan who had ascended to the presidency after John F. Kennedy was slain in 1963. Bobby Kennedy — a smaller, more intense, less patient, "hotter"

version of his older brother — had lived uncomplainingly in Jack Kennedy's shadow, doing his political dirty work, deflecting (sometimes brutally) his critics, considering himself the subordinate willing and able to take many of the hits directed at the man out front.

But now it was 1968, nearly five years after his brother's death, and the war John Kennedy had escalated had become to Robert Kennedy a horror without a foreseeable end. Bobby had long since decided that he would seek the presidency someday, which is why he was subjecting himself to the torpor of serving in the United States Senate. That glacial, tradition-encrusted institution was for him an unavoidable way station to the White House. But it didn't seem that his bid to restore what Jackie Kennedy had mythologized as Camelot could come to pass until 1972 at the earliest. Even if the voters should accede sooner to a revival of the Kennedy dynasty, the boss-controlled Democratic party would not. It was all but universally thought that Bobby Kennedy would have to wait.

But waiting was not something that Bobby did well. As bombs rained, to little effect, on jungle-hardened troops and Vietnamese villages, much of the world looked on aghast at mighty America sinking into Asian quicksand. A nation whose previous wartime ventures had evoked chiefly patriotic fervor was now becoming more and more disenchanted. Television was bringing war into living rooms for the first time, and decent Americans who had never before doubted their country's rectitude now had questions to ask: What are we fighting for? How long must Americans go on killing and being killed eleven thousand miles away? What is it to us if South Vietnam has a Communist government? What is the price? Thousands of American youth fled to

At a campaign dinner in Ohio
in 1966, RFK stands before
a photograph of his brother.

Canada or Sweden to avoid the draft. Many others sought
refuge in educational deferments. Dan Quayle, destined to
become vice president after the Republican sweep of the
1988 election, spent the war years close to home as an
Indiana national guardsman.

In 1965, Robert Kennedy went public with his doubts
about the war. A year later his skepticism was being frequently expressed, and in 1967 it was written in *Time* and
elsewhere that he had "crossed the Rubicon" by urging a
negotiated settlement, a policy Johnson described as "cut
and run." Still, Kennedy shrank from the one step — openly
challenging Lyndon Johnson — that would have solidified
antiwar opposition. Eugene McCarthy, a Democratic senator barely known outside his home state of Minnesota and
Washington, D.C., urged Kennedy to run for the nomination. Convinced that a Kennedy-Johnson battle would split
the party and the country and that Johnson would prevail
against a revival of the dynasty, Kennedy demurred. So, in
1967, McCarthy took on the fight himself.

Campaigning primarily on college campuses, where concerned students listened attentively, McCarthy was soon
peeling back the layers of hopelessness — proving that America was receptive to honest debate and that opposition to
U.S. involvement in a faraway war was not automatically
discounted as traitorous. He entered the New Hampshire
primary of March 1968 and came away with 41.9 percent
of the vote. Although the hawkish Johnson received more
than 49 percent as a write-in candidate, McCarthy has
always been regarded as the winner of that race. In an epic
sense, he was.

Once Gene McCarthy had blazed the trail, Bobby swiftly
agreed to enter the race. The declaration of his candidacy

A rare quiet moment aboard
a nearly empty plane.

During his presidential campaigns,
JFK gave away tie clips shaped like
PT boats, as does Bobby in 1966.

Bobby frequently used
the Kennedys' private
plane, *The Caroline*,
for political trips.

touched off a frenzy at the White House and dealt a blow to the less well known McCarthy. Pragmatists of the antiwar movement knew that neither man was likely to wrest the nomination from Lyndon Johnson. But if by some miracle it could be done, Kennedy, not McCarthy, would do it. Still, the unexpected challenge by the supposedly most arrogant of the Kennedys embittered McCarthy and his supporters.

Bobby's reputation for ruthlessness had been born of his unrelenting pursuit of the corrupt Teamsters union boss, Jimmy Hoffa; his midnight dispatch of FBI agents to reporters' homes during a domestic steel crisis; and his unforgiving interrogation of witnesses as a staff attorney for Joe McCarthy's Senate investigations subcommittee. Kennedy seemed to validate the worst that had been said about him when he stepped into the spotlight Eugene McCarthy had deservedly attracted.

Weeks later, Robert Kennedy was to explain that it had become "unmistakably clear to me that so long as Lyndon B. Johnson was president, our Vietnam policy would consist only of more war, more troops, more killing, and more senseless destruction of the country we were supposedly there to save." Implicit in his comment: McCarthy as challenger meant four more years of Lyndon Johnson, four more years of war.

As for running in 1968, the motive Kennedy expressed was probably true. But, as has been said earlier, Robert Kennedy's yearning to become president of the United States predated his declaration of candidacy. Jack Kennedy used to joke in public about "Bobby's turn," which would come after — possibly immediately after — Jack's second term. Bobby had been trying to wait for the right moment in his bid for succession, but he felt compelled by the circumstances to take action.

The premature end to Camelot had left Kennedy idolators feeling cheated. Great, and perhaps inflated, expectations had gone unfulfilled. However large or minimal his achievements, Jack Kennedy had stimulated the nation and convinced millions of Americans that their lives and their nation could be better. He expected to be in the White House for eight years. He lived there just short of three. During his term, he moved from opportunism to idealism, nudged by his younger brother, the attorney general. Bobby combined a sure sense of practical politics with a nascent compassion. As head of the Justice Department, he acquired a keen interest in the civil rights division. The integration of southern schools and colleges was rending the nation. It was Bobby, his brother's firm and collected field marshal, who convinced the president that the administration could not retreat in the face of southern bigotry — much of it official by way of George Wallace and Ross Barnett, the segregationist governors of Alabama and Mississippi. Robert Kennedy was a major player in every crisis of his brother's administration. The crucial decision of the Cuban missile crisis — to ignore Khrushchev's belligerent second note and respond to his less-heated initial proposal — was Bobby's. He forced a reluctant FBI director, J. Edgar Hoover, to confront organized crime. A neophyte when appointed, Robert Kennedy was by 1968 a successful, seasoned, battle-tested public official, as well equipped for the presidency as Hubert Humphrey or Nixon and far more fit than McCarthy.

Bobby had been devastated by his brother's murder and the end of their partnership. He brooded for months — the tumultuous and tragic past filled his thoughts, leaving precious little room for weighing the future. Intimate friends said he didn't seem to care. Yet not caring was alien to the intensely driven third son of Joseph P. Kennedy. Urged on

Kids running alongside RFK's convertible while he campaigns
for Governor G. Mennen ("Soapy") Williams's Senate
race in Michigan, 1966.

by Kennedy restorationists, RFK had let it be known that he would be willing to run as Lyndon Johnson's vice president in 1964, thus positioning himself for the presidency in 1972. In this he failed to reckon with LBJ, whose disdain for the Kennedys in general was exceeded only by his hatred of Bobby in particular. When Johnson spurned his overture, Bobby said, "I think I could have helped you." But Johnson won the 1964 election without any Kennedy help, teaming with Hubert Humphrey for the greatest landslide up to that point in the history of U.S. presidential elections.

Robert Kennedy was on the ballot that year, too, but only in a senatorial race in New York State, where he did not live and where he was denounced as a carpetbagger. He won a seat in the U.S. Senate, even though he ran six hundred thousand votes behind the Johnson-Humphrey ticket. No matter. He had a forum, and his goal was firmly fixed: the presidency in 1972. "It was never contemplated," said his close aide Frank Mankiewicz, "that Bobby would become president pro tem of the Senate" (an honorific conferred on the longest-serving senator of the party controlling the Senate).

This, his first election to public office, and the campaign that preceded it gave Bobby confidence. His renown, the reverence for his dead brother, the passions he stirred, and the principles he stood for guaranteed huge crowds. Most important, he learned how to handle those crowds — to deflect hecklers and to soften antagonists, chiefly through self-deprecating humor. At times — clothes rumpled, lengthening hair askew, grasping a forest of outstretched hands, standing atop a convertible as his fans tried to touch him — he resembled a rock star more than a political candidate. As planned, the 1964 senatorial race in New York was a rehearsal for a Kennedy presidential bid. Somewhat to his own

Campaigning in Michigan for "Soapy" Williams
(in bow tie), RFK draws most of the attention.

surprise, and to that of the prematurely displaced denizens of Camelot, Robert Kennedy proved to be an adept campaigner. Previously he had toiled chiefly behind the scenes, where his brusque manner and blunt talk offended some loyalists, but he seemed to shed his hard edges on the stump. He began to display in public an earnestness and compassion theretofore known only to his intimates. Thoughts among Kennedy followers that Bobby wasn't up to the task receded, and they began to tell each other that they could barely wait for 1972. As it happened, they didn't have to.

In the Senate, Robert Kennedy used his committee assignments to awaken the nation to the plight of its impoverished—in urban ghettos, in the Mississippi Delta, in Appalachia, and on the tenant farms and Indian reservations of the South and the West. Although slow to emerge emotionally from what he referred to as "the events of November 1963," when he did he assumed full command of the Kennedy clan, as befit the oldest surviving son. He was in an anomalous situation regarding Lyndon Johnson, urging a negotiated end to the war and yet claiming to support the warring Johnson for re-election in 1968. The White House eyed Kennedy with a mixture of disdain and awe. His speeches almost invariably were reported on page one, at home and abroad. Vice President Hubert Humphrey groused, after one Kennedy speech on urban problems, "I could say the same thing and wind up with one paragraph. Bobby says it and the *New York Times* runs the text." Johnson, meanwhile, became convinced that Kennedy would run against him in 1968, even though Larry O'Brien, a JFK supporter now in Johnson's cabinet, and a bridge between the two factions, assured the president that Bobby would wait until 1972. McCarthy's "victory" in New Hampshire changed all that.

And so the Last Campaign began. Standing in the ornate Senate Caucus Room, where John F. Kennedy had declared his underdog candidacy in early 1960, Bobby Kennedy knew that his only path to the White House would be the one his brother had blazed—the primaries. Only by winning primaries convincingly would Bobby Kennedy be able to wrest the nomination from the incumbent, whose backers included most of the Democratic senators (only brother Ted and George McGovern of South Dakota supported RFK) and most Democratic governors and mayors—the party establishment.

In the crowded Caucus Room, Kennedy, somehow looking even smaller and thinner than usual, told the nation he would run "to propose new policies." He added, "I cannot stand aside from the contest that will decide our nation's future." Robert Kennedy would run because he had to.

"He Looks Like a Little Kid"

You see the slight figure, the shy, self-conscious wave of the hand, the shoulders that slope, the hair that loses out to the breeze. Inevitably one of the curious will say, "He looks like a little kid."

His Harvard accent evokes a pleasanter time, a reminder of his brother's delightful presidential style. "Cuber," he calls Cuba, and when the crowd laughs he kids himself about it. His brother said "Cuber," too. "We can do bettah," the candidate repeats, over and over, rekindling a hope many haven't felt since JFK's death in 1963. Bobby Kennedy campaigning for president is bright, warm, gentle. He can laugh at himself. Why do magazines and newspapers and commentators call him "ruthless"?

One appealing thing about this Kennedy is that anyone can understand him. He's a senator, but he doesn't speak "senatorialese." He doesn't say that he sponsored the revised amendment to article ten, section three, of the farm bill; instead, he speaks clearly and passionately about the indecency of war. Never before has a political candidate made the misery of the ghetto seem so real. He inspires belief, even though he's short on details and admits he doesn't have all the answers. At least he talks about finding solutions instead of citing depressing warnings about more austerity and more taxes and more troops that mean more deaths. He talks of better days.

Deep down, you know that the past wasn't as pleasant as Robert Francis Kennedy would have you remember it and that the future may not be as bright as he paints it. But right now Bobby Kennedy symbolizes the best of two worlds — the one that never was and the one that never will be. They're both better to contemplate than the world that is.

In New York State, in 1964, the crowds were simply tremendous, larger than in any senate campaign in memory. Bobby told friends, "They aren't there for me — they're there for him," meaning President Kennedy. And to an extent that was true. Not everyone was friendly. Some of the signs said "Carpetbagger" and "Kennedy Go Home," "Bobby Ain't Jack" and "Democrats for Keating." Bobby was running against Kenneth Keating, the moderate Republican incumbent, and was clearly planning to use the job as a stepping-stone to the one he really wanted. Bobby and his handlers knew this race would be tough. But the outpouring wasn't all for Jack; Bobby had plenty of fans himself.

At first shy and uncomfortable in the role of candidate, this natural-born campaigner soon realized his talent with

Presidential candidate Robert F. Kennedy at a midwestern airport.

13

Asked to help Paul Douglas with his Senate race in Illinois,
Bobby flies to Chicago and is greeted at the airport by former
JFK supporter Mayor Richard Daley (left).

Vice President Hubert Humphrey deals with hecklers
at 1966 Jefferson-Jackson Day dinner while
Bobby signs autographs.

crowds. When someone shouted, "We don't want you, Kennedy," he would reply, "This is a difficult campaign, and I knew it would be. I never expected it to be unanimous." People laughed, and some who came to a rally out of curiosity admitted that Bobby Kennedy didn't seem as ruthless as they had heard he was. Still, they felt uneasy about an intruder coming into the state and knocking off old Ken Keating, who was at least a New Yorker and a decent senator. On election day, RFK won "the only poll that counts," starting him on his seemingly inevitable path to the White House.

As the line begins to form for a second Kennedy presidency, another line — to resist it — takes shape. In 1966, Robert Kennedy's support is sought in the campaigns of G. Mennen ("Soapy") Williams in Michigan, Edmund G. ("Pat") Brown in California, Paul Douglas in Illinois, and by other Democrats running for office east, north, and west. In the South, however, where as attorney general he had enforced court-ordered school integration, RFK is thought not to be too popular.

The war in Vietnam has become a major issue, and Kennedy has "crossed the Rubicon" with his call for a negotiated settlement, which Johnson derides. Democrats loyal to the president warn of a "Kennedy dynasty" in the making, but Bobby insists that he intends to remain a senator and to support the Johnson-Humphrey ticket in 1968. Crowds boo and hiss when he says this, and in private he is pained, because he abhors Johnson's hawkishness on Vietnam but feels powerless to counter it. A challenge would be seen as Kennedy versus Johnson, not peace versus war.

The antiwar movement continues to grow. Where once only bold senators like J. William Fulbright of Arkansas and Wayne Morse of Oregon dared be associated with it, now Robert Kennedy has given the protest movement new respectability. Senators Eugene McCarthy and George McGovern, from America's heartland — Minnesota and South Dakota — join in, convinced that Johnson can be toppled and the war ended if Bobby Kennedy will challenge him in 1968. But the powerful party bosses still support Johnson, believing that the country — except for a small group of bearded, beaded, sandal-clad "radicals" — wants to win the war. To what end, Kennedy muses in private, should he seek the presidency? To be condemned as the party wrecker, the traitor who tried to destroy his brother's successor? What power would he have then to help end the war?

"Bobby Ain't Jack"

Comparisons were inevitable. Bobby Kennedy was less gracious, not so handsome, shorter, and much less outgoing than his older brother. Upon meeting someone new, John Kennedy appeared genuinely delighted; the smile was ready, the arm was outstretched. If the stranger was a local pol, John Kennedy probably had been briefed and remembered (like many successful politicians, he had a prodigious memory) some little fact: "Oh, yes, you're in the state legislature." Bobby often seemed cold by comparison, but he wasn't — just noncommittal. His steely stare was absolutely neutral. Even though you might be willing to walk through walls for him, he would reserve judgment until you had done so — or tried to. Then Bobby's defenses would melt, and you knew he would walk through walls for you, too.

Constantly being compared to his brother had its downside, especially since JFK's death had raised the president to

President Lyndon Johnson delivers a speech from the presidential limousine
in Bay Ridge, Brooklyn, at the dedication of the Verrazano Narrows Bridge in 1966.
RFK, the junior senator from New York, shakes hands at the other end of the car.

Later that day, as Johnson
speaks, Bobby's attitude toward
the president is clear.

In Brooklyn, a police squad
escorts RFK through the crowd.

a saintly status that was hard to live up to. Also, there was the dynasty backlash for Bobby to worry about: Were the Kennedys intent on establishing themselves as American royalty? If Bobby should become president, who next? Teddy? And then the next generation?

But what chiefly concerned Bobby about the comparisons was that this wasn't his brother's era any longer. The problems were different, and so were the tools for attacking them. As a senator, Bobby had tried to distinguish himself from Jack, and as president—if it came to that—he would be different, too. Clearly, on key issues like Vietnam, a continued Lyndon Johnson presidency would more closely resemble Jack Kennedy's New Frontier than would a Bobby Kennedy administration. The gulf would be wide, too, on how to attack urban problems and on much else. Bobby Kennedy could not run as John Kennedy's clone. Yet, wherever he spoke to gatherings of Democrats, there were the gigantic portraits of Jack, the introductions of "the junior senator from the state of New York, brother of the late president. . . ." Bobby never ceased being proud of Jack's legacy, but now he was trying to establish his own. Whenever possible he would distance himself from his brother's portrait, frustrating photographers but making a statement. More often, however, Jack on film smiled down from behind the speaker's dais. When the occasional "Bobby Ain't Jack" sign would turn up in a crowd, aides thought they could hear Bobby mutter, under his breath, "I'm not trying to be." One time, in Grand Rapids, Michigan, a double line of high-school drum majorettes chanted over and over, "JFK in '68," until finally one of them, horror-stricken, clapped her hand over her mouth and succeeded in altering the chant to "RFK in '68."

Crush at the edge of a stage in Iowa.

And then there was Johnson. After Jack Kennedy decided that it was a mistake to have chosen Lyndon Johnson as his running mate in 1960, it was Bobby who had to tell the Texan he was off the ticket — just moments before Jack changed his mind again. By 1964, Bobby's differences with President Johnson were chiefly a mutual hatred and did not yet include the war. "Bobby," old Joe Kennedy is reported to have said, admiringly, "hates just the way I do." In regard to Lyndon Johnson, the statement was no doubt true.

Insecure even after winning a new term in his own right, Johnson took personally Robert Kennedy's increasingly violent thrusts at Johnsonian war policy. When the two men shared the spotlight at political rallies or other gatherings, the tension was palpable. Johnson made feeble attempts at surface affability; Kennedy could not conceal his worsening contempt for the president if he tried — and he didn't try. He was undeniably rude, often greeting well-wishers as the president was introduced or paying little attention when he spoke.

When Johnson was John Kennedy's vice president he was known to the White House staff as "Uncle Cornpone," and that is how Bobby and his followers viewed him now — as someone hopelessly wedded to southern rural politics, locked into the past. "He doesn't understand that this is a new age," said one New Frontiersman anxious for Robert Kennedy — who did understand — to mount a challenge. "LBJ'll campaign as if it's 1964, or even 1960, and that's why he can be beaten."

Robert Kennedy's juices were flowing. A good excuse might have brought him into the race. But 1967 passed, and evidently no excuse had been good enough.

A wave good-bye from the steps of a plane.

THE LAST CAMPAIGN

Testing the Waters

Bobby Kennedy always drew a crowd, from the 1964 Senate campaign to the Democratic primaries of 1968. Over and over, *Life* staff photographer Bill Eppridge's camera caught the looks of ecstasy and enthrallment on the faces of those who crowded around Bobby Kennedy. It was always the same scene — chaos, screams, a sea of outstretched hands, people waiting hours just to glimpse him. But would this translate into votes? There was the middle-aged woman on an American Airlines flight who, noticing that champagne had been served in the first-class cabin, asked the stewardess for Kennedy's empty bottle. The stewardess told her, "The senator didn't have any. But you must really like him." Replied the woman, "I do. But I'm not going to vote for him."

More than any political figure of his era, Bobby Kennedy could stir emotional

responses from spectators. People—mostly young, but some old—would wait hours to try to touch him or get a peek at him. Mayors and governors and congressmen stayed clear of Kennedy rallies, however, and they were the ones who would be delegates at future Democratic national conventions.

They knew instinctively—and if they did not know they were told—that President Johnson would regard even courtesy appearances with his rival as rank disloyalty. And Johnson's memory was long, meaning that delegates would not vote for Kennedy unless he could prove that his popular support was overwhelming. So it was to the people that Kennedy took his case.

The public's receptiveness to Bobby's message surprised him. He quickly realized that the narrow vein he had hoped to tap was already a mother lode. Many Americans, with their first front-row seats for a political campaign—television was in 75.3 million homes in 1968, compared to only 51.7 million in 1960—were startled by the antiwar sentiments RFK stirred at his outdoor rallies. Others had ceased debating whether the war was right or wrong. All they wanted was out. The objectives of that faraway jungle war may have been noble, but the price had become too high. Bobby Kennedy had once wondered if his comment that "not in one hundred years has our country been so divided" was hyperbolic; it no longer seemed so. Where in early speeches he had cautiously tested the waters of discontent, now he often threw away his prepared text and waded into a harsh condemnation of what he regarded as the national folly. John Glenn, the famous astronaut, had been traveling with Bobby, telling audiences that "America needs someone who will tell it like it is" and that only Robert Kennedy could fulfill that role.

Hecklers appeared, but not as often as Kennedy had expected—perhaps because he had become so adept at handling them. At Vanderbilt University, in Tennessee, a skeptic taunted the candidate by confronting him with his 1962 statement that America would stay in Vietnam "until we win." Conceded Kennedy, "I made a mistake in 1962. I would feel better if President Johnson would admit he made a mistake, too." The applause was thunderous.

Another heckler, this one a black student at Ball State University, in Indiana, unknowingly contributed to one of the startling coincidences of presidential politics. Stocky and broad shouldered, the student scoffed at Kennedy's "platitudes" about the need for whites and blacks to live together harmoniously. Scornfully, he asked, "Do you really believe that the white population wants this?" Replied Kennedy, "Yes. Of course, there are hotheads, white and black." But the majority of both races are "anxious to do what is right and what is just." It was 6:45 P.M., eastern standard time, on April 4, 1968. Neither the questioner nor Robert Kennedy could know that Martin Luther King, Jr., lay dying on a motel balcony in Memphis, victim of one of those "hotheads."

Visibly shaken when informed of King's death, Kennedy flew to Indianapolis and, despite warnings, insisted on making his scheduled speech to a nearly all-black audience gathered on an outdoor basketball court. It was Robert Kennedy at his most eloquent and most real. "I have bad news for you," he began, sensing that his listeners were unaware of the assassination, "for all of our fellow citizens, and people who love peace all over the world, and that is that Martin Luther King was shot and killed tonight." Someone cried out, "Oh, Jesus!" and there were a few shouts of "black power" before Kennedy continued, saying, in part:

The faces of women always reveal
a particular appreciation of RFK.

Cheerleader performs onstage
at a Democratic rally, 1966.

"In this difficult day, in this difficult time for the United States, it is perhaps well to ask what kind of nation we are and what direction we want to move in. For those of you who are black — considering the evidence there evidently is that there were white people who were responsible — you can be filled with bitterness, with hatred, and a desire for revenge. We can move in that direction as a country, in great polarization — black people amongst black, white people amongst white, filled with hatred toward one another.

"Or we can make an effort, as Martin Luther King did, to understand and to comprehend and to replace that violence, that stain of bloodshed that has spread across our land, with an effort to understand, with compassion and love.

"For those of you who are black and are tempted to be filled with hatred and distrust at the injustice of such an act, against all white people, I can only say that I feel in my own heart the same kind of feeling. I had a member of my family killed, but he was killed by a white man. But we have to make an effort . . . to understand, to go beyond these rather difficult times."

Aware that he had begun to repeat himself, Kennedy resorted to quoting Aeschylus: "'In our sleep, pain which cannot forget falls drop by drop upon the heart until, in our own despair, against our will, comes wisdom through the awful grace of God.'" He ended with "Let us dedicate ourselves to what the Greeks wrote so many years ago: to tame the savageness of man and to make gentle the life of this world. Let us dedicate ourselves to that, and say a prayer for our country and for our people." His audience, hushed while he spoke, applauded and cheered him warmly, then gathered around him.

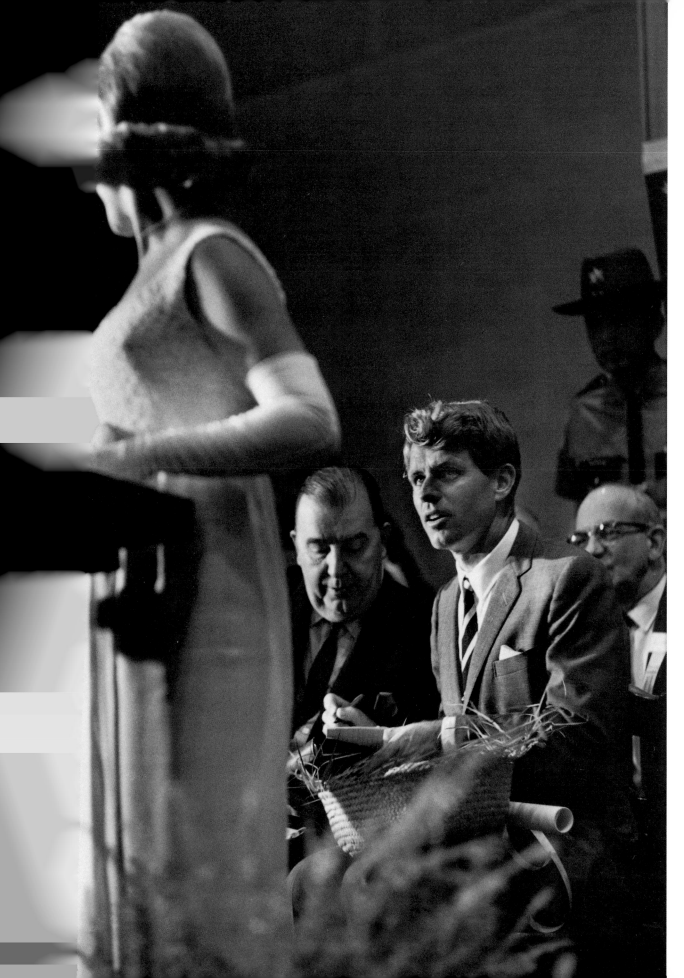

At a West Virginia rally, seated next to
Senator Jennings Randolph, RFK is introduced
by a local beauty queen.

LBJ Goes Away

Long on popular appeal but acutely short of convention delegates, the Bobby Kennedy campaign was beginning to flounder when in late March it received a jolting mid-course correction from the most unexpected source: Lyndon Johnson. As Kennedy and his wife, Ethel, some of their brood, and the huge entourage of press and hangers-on soaked up the sun in Phoenix, word came from Washington that the president had asked the networks for time to address the nation. Would he order a resumption of the bombing of North Vietnam? Would he float a peace feeler? Whatever it was, Kennedy could not make a move until he knew. The frenetic campaign came to a halt, and the candidate flew to New York, intending to watch Lyndon Johnson on television like everyone else. By the time the plane had landed and the president had finished speaking, the whole political land-scape had changed.

Lyndon Johnson had declared himself finished with pol-itics: "I shall not seek, and I will not accept, the nomination of my party for another term as your president." He would devote his remaining months in office to the war that had destroyed his presidency and ripped the country apart. He would try to negotiate a peaceful settlement, which was what Bobby Kennedy and, before him, Gene McCarthy had been campaigning for. The development was so startling, so un-Johnsonian. You can never unseat a sitting president of your own party, Kennedy had been told, and now he and McCarthy had done just that, mobilizing a latent antiwar sentiment so pervasive that no president could have tamed it. Johnson had tried to do so, and Nixon and Ford would try, too, but Americans had gotten ahead of their leaders. The

Moments after this photograph is taken at an airport reception, the crowd pushes the fence down.

36

Bobby's fondness for kids was reciprocated. Here, a boy at a rally in Michigan.

At an airport, a man presents his two grandsons. After a bit of discussion, a friendly tweak of the ear brings a delighted yelp.

At the foot of the stage, a group of awed children

wait in hopes of an autograph.

people knew what presidents had still to learn: that Vietnam could not be "won" and that it was best to get out — "honorably" if possible, any other way if not.

A virtual prisoner in the White House, Johnson could not step outside or tune in his television without hearing the dreaded chant "Hey, hey, LBJ, how many kids did you kill today?" He spoke little in public, and then mainly on military bases, where he could distance himself from the angry and ubiquitous protesters. Still, no one had imagined that this proud man might step down, particularly when the person likeliest to step up was his roundly hated rival, Robert Kennedy. But LBJ, after his "loss" to McCarthy in New Hampshire, was about to lose to him for real in Wisconsin, where, Larry O'Brien had told Johnson, he would be lucky to get one-third of the votes. (Kennedy had missed the Wisconsin filing deadline and was urging support of McCarthy.) A stinging primary defeat was a humiliation Lyndon Baines Johnson could not abide, so he made his dramatic withdrawal from the presidential race the weekend before the Wisconsin primary.

No longer could Kennedy campaign against President Johnson, whose destruction he had hastened. Nor could he continue to focus on the war — Johnson to all appearances was at least trying to find a way out. Even with the incumbent no longer a factor, Robert Kennedy was not the front-runner, and the Democratic party bosses were more determined than ever to block him. Their choice — and LBJ's — was Vice President Hubert Humphrey, an old-fashioned pol but one who was impossible to hate. Humphrey suited not only the party bosses but those Democrats and independents who found Kennedy too "hot" and independent for their taste. Humphrey could also avoid a

A drive in Virginia with son Max and dog, Freckles.

Flying to a political rally in 1966, Bobby plans
strategy with aides as reporters look on.

popularity test against Bobby Kennedy, if he chose, simply by avoiding all the remaining primaries and winning the nomination by capturing the votes of delegates pledged to Johnson. More than ever, Kennedy's task was the same as his brother's had been in 1960 — to win over delegates by convincing them that he could beat Nixon in November. With the despised and discredited Lyndon Johnson no longer providing a large and inviting target, this would be no small task.

The Entourage

"The Ruthless Cannonball" (sung to the tune of "The Wabash Cannonball" by reporters covering the Kennedy campaign in Indiana):

> Oh listen to the speeches that baffle, beef and bore
> As he waffles through the woodlands, and slides along
>   the shore.
> He's the politician who is touched by one and all.
> He's the demon driver of the Ruthless Cannonball.

And the concluding verse:

> So here's to Ruthless Robert, may his name forever stand,
> To be feared and genuflected at by pols across the land.
> Old Ho Chi Minh is cheering, and though it may appall,
> He's whizzing to the White House on the Ruthless
>   Cannonball.

Perhaps because the campaign was nonstop, with people thrown together from one dawn until the next, a familial camaraderie developed, which included the candidate and his wife. Bobby Kennedy was virtually omnipresent among the staff and the journalists — on the campaign plane, in motels and restaurants, at bars, in swimming pools. When reporters received queries from their home offices, or when photo editors forwarded special picture requests, there was no red tape. As often as not, the question could be put directly to the candidate, seated across the aisle of the plane, bus, or train or down a few rows. On the few occasions when he was temporarily tied up with his speech writers or campaign strategists, someone on the huge Kennedy staff could be instantly located. There was no room or inclination for formality on the train called "The Ruthless Cannonball" or on any of the other conveyances utilized on the campaign trail. Instead of dour secret-service agents menacingly surrounding the candidate on every trip, Kennedy usually sat briefly with his foremost adviser, Fred Dutton, and then roamed the aircraft or train. His single bodyguard, a huge former FBI agent named Bill Barry, was happy to allow full access. Most often, a reporter requesting an interview would be invited to sit with the candidate, who, sipping a Jack Daniels on the rocks at the end of a hard day, would comment on any subject — though carefully specifying "that's not for attribution" when the conversation turned to his political rivals or his detailed strategy. The intimacy did not immunize the campaign from negative coverage, but it no doubt had some effect. Still, the occasional tough story was accepted as a given by the candidate and his staff. An exception was Ethel Kennedy, who once folded up a *Washington Post* containing a harsh critique of her husband and whacked its author, Richard Harwood, on the head. She was not being entirely playful.

One Saturday morning, while covering the campaign for *Time* magazine, I found Robert Kennedy alone in a private dining car during a whistle-stop train ride from Cheyenne, Wyoming, to Omaha, Nebraska. He was dwarfed by the huge table at which he was sitting, looking strangely solitary without crowds, cameras, aides, reporters. Bobby Kennedy was entitled to a peaceful moment, but somehow he didn't seem to want it. He bade me sit down, and the conversation began with my banal and predictable "Well, how's it going?"

Replied Kennedy, "I don't think I'm tired. People say I look tired. But I really think it's something else. You know — I'd really rather be doing other things [than campaigning].

"But you have to campaign if you want to win. Small towns, for instance. People in Kimball and Sydney appreciate your coming there. I guess Gene McCarthy will try to do it in the next few days on television. Maybe he can turn things around. He's good on television. But I still think it means something if people can see you in person.

"The reason for the difference in our campaigns? I don't know about him, but I really want this [the presidency]. I'm willing to break my neck to get it, too." Then, after a pause: "I don't know what I'll do if I'm not elected."

Wasn't he frightened by the enormity of the presidency?

"Awed? No. Frightened? Not that, either. I want to do things. I think there are a lot of things that can be done. I think I could bring bright people into government with me — people with ideas. We can harness the good that is within people with programs like the Peace Corps and Vista. There's a lot of good in this country that ought to be harnessed. . . . The enormity of the presidency doesn't worry me. I don't think I could face a crisis worse than the Cuban missile crisis."

What about a major domestic crisis?

"I think I can work with the Negroes as well as anyone can. I think I can get them to do things, to work together with the whites. You know, the Negroes and the poor — they aren't very numerous. But their situation is what's wrong with the country. Scotty Reston [*New York Times* columnist James Reston] says Hubert Humphrey is in the best position to unify the party and the country. But he's not talking about what the real divisions are. To bring labor and business together isn't the problem. They're already together. All the establishments are together — business, labor, politics. The alienated are the young and the poor and the Negroes. The problem is to end those divisions."

The train began to slow down for another whistle-stop, another speech. Robert Kennedy stood up and said, "I'd like to try."

With the Kennedy money, the loyalty the family had always commanded, and the cross-country networks established during John F. Kennedy's presidential campaign, Bobby Kennedy had a huge reservoir of talent to tap in his bid for the presidential nomination. In addition, there were his own and brother Ted's Senate staffs, the use of which triggered a brief flurry in the press before the staffers were removed from the Senate payroll and paid from campaign funds. By far the greatest influences on Robert Kennedy were Fred Dutton, a Californian who had served in the State Department after helping in Jack Kennedy's 1960 campaign, and Adam Walinsky, a young, long-haired opponent of the war in Vietnam. Dutton, quiet and self-effacing, older than the candidate, was a master political strategist and analyst who had the candidate's ear every day of the campaign. Walinsky,

Aboard another flight, with his press secretary, Frank Mankiewicz.

A very young photographer, homemade press card in hat.

Photographer Bert Berensky of *Time*.

Steve Shapiro of Black Star Picture Agency photographs Bobby in his car.

A newspaper photographer takes hands off the wheel and eyes off the road to snap pictures.

1968: At the beginning of the presidential campaign, in Logansport,
Indiana, police are very much on the alert.

Policeman with high-powered rifle
on a nearby rooftop.

Controlling the crowds.

whose hippie-ish appearance during his visits to Kennedy on the floor of the Senate triggered consternation in some of the more sedate members, had been the greatest single influence on Kennedy's change of heart and mind on the Vietnam War.

A brilliant lawyer, Walinsky, then thirty-one, was the campaign's foremost speech writer and — unjustly — a major source of friction. His demeanor bespoke revolution. Despite his Italian-cut suits, button-down collars, striped shirts, and cuffless trousers, his hair was long, and, in his rare idle moments, he played the guitar. He formed a duet with an even younger speech writer, Jeff Greenfield, later a political analyst for ABC. Walinsky, without trying, annoyed anyone with a traditional bent and was automatically labeled in the press as a "new leftist," which he was not. (In later years, Walinsky was an admirer of Ronald Reagan, and he actively supported a conservative Republican candidate for governor of his home state, New York.) Abrasive and unyielding, Walinsky was a major annoyance to the Jack Kennedy legatees working on Bobby's campaign, but pleas that he be dropped went unheeded. The candidate knew that he had no more valuable adviser or skilled speech writer. The Robert Kennedy book *To Seek a Newer World* owed much to Walinsky's work, as the senator wrote in his acknowledgments.

Bobby Kennedy, always intrigued by new ideas, had drawn some genuine "new leftists" into his inner circle, the best known being writers Jack Newfield and Pete Hamill. But they were quietly dropped when the presidential campaign began — at least in part because old Kennedy hands like Ted Sorensen and Pierre Salinger could not abide them. They didn't suit the measured image the candidate was obliged to project.

Sorensen and Dick Goodwin also did some speech writ-

ing for Bobby, but Goodwin's reputation suffered from his having flitted from JFK to Lyndon Johnson to Eugene McCarthy and then to Bobby. He acquired the scornful label of "Have-typewriter-will-travel Goodwin." But he and Sorensen melded reasonably well with Walinsky. The expected friction between Salinger, JFK's portly press secretary, and Frank Mankiewicz, whom Bobby had plucked from the Peace Corps to handle his press operation, did not develop. That potentially prickly rivalry was averted when Salinger took over the Washington headquarters press office while Mankiewicz spent nearly full time traveling with the candidate. A rivalry that did flourish involved two JFK loyalists, Larry O'Brien and Kenny O'Donnell. ("They speak but don't communicate," Bobby Kennedy observed.)

As always, there was plenty of family involved in the campaign. Steve Smith, the handsome husband of Bobby's youngest sister, Jean, handled fund-raising. Ted Kennedy worked on anti-Bobby politicians in the nonprimary states, without much success, noting on one occasion that he had learned "nobody is neutral about Robert Kennedy." Bobby's wife, Ethel, traveled with the campaign when her role as mother of ten (soon to be eleven) allowed, and there were drop-in visits by mother Rose, sisters Eunice Shriver, Pat Lawford, and Jean Smith, and sister-in-law Joan Kennedy. At various stages of the campaign, some glamorous Kennedy hangers-on came aboard the campaign plane, including former astronaut John Glenn and Rene Carpenter, the wife of another space explorer, each serving as a reminder of the John F. Kennedy administration's adventurousness. Athletes were always welcome, among them Stan Musial, Roosevelt Grier, Rafer Johnson, Bill Russell, Bob Cousy, and Hank Aaron.

Last car of the Kennedy campaign train, traveling through Indiana. The senator, Ethel, and David shake hands with the crowd.

52

Ethel watches as children run after
the departing campaign train.

Catholic school students line the road to catch a glimpse
of the candidate in Indiana.

The Defanging

By the time Bobby Kennedy decided to run for president, his image as a ruthless prosecutor-turned-politician had begun to soften. All but the most biased observers had conceded that his concern for the underprivileged was genuine. But he could not avoid reviving accusations of opportunism when he plunged in on Eugene McCarthy at the very moment of the Minnesotan's psychological challenge to Lyndon Johnson — a challenge Bobby had been unwilling to mount despite months of importunings.

Aware that Bobby haters were not amenable to persuasion, his advisers nonetheless felt that the fable of the unmerciful Kennedy brother had to be dispelled among the general public. They were confident that thousands of the "just curious" would turn out to gawk at the famed and controversial candidate, and they wanted these potential converts to experience the Bobby Kennedy they knew — the warmhearted and delightfully witty father of ten, the enemy of privation, the seeker of justice, the spontaneous jokester. Who could find a man who told jokes on himself cold and ruthless?

His skill at both planned and spontaneous banter exceeded all expectations. When one overall-clad farmer at a Kennedy rally in Tecumseh, Nebraska, finally brought his laughter under control, he told a reporter, "Seems to me he sort of respects our intelligence."

In Tecumseh, for example, the wind had blown a tiny piece of paper from the lectern. "That's my farm program!" Kennedy exclaimed in mock alarm. "Give it back, quickly!" The audience, deep in Nebraska farm country, laughed appreciatively. It did so again when Bobby joshed, "My mother told me I should run for president of the United States. Do

Bobby tells a joke.

55

you know why? She said that if you do, then you can enter the Nebraska primary, and then you can come to Tecumseh." Laughter and groans.

In several farm communities, Kennedy announced, "Other candidates will be coming through here, telling you how much they will do for the farmer. I'm already doing more for the farmer than any of them. I am doing more for the farm economy than any candidate, Republican or Democrat, and if you don't believe me, just look down my breakfast table or my lunch table any day of the week. We are consuming more milk and more bread and more eggs — doing more for farm consumption — than the family of any other candidate. I challenge the other two Democrats to do as well by the date of the primary, and I challenge Richard Nixon to do as well by November." (At one stop in Nebraska, after this litany, a farmer called out, "We grow corn around here." Kennedy shot back, "We had corn for dinner last night.")

During a stop at San Jose College, in California, chimes rang out in mid speech, drowning Kennedy's words. When the din faded the candidate deadpanned, "Ronald Reagan, I'll get even with you." (Reagan was then the Republican governor of California.)

In Richmond, Indiana, a campaign staffer's words were accidentally picked up by the loudspeaker system. "Will all drivers report to their cars," she said. Kennedy: "She could tell by my voice I was reaching a conclusion."

To students everywhere, Bobby joked, "No matter who you vote for eventually, I want you to remember that it was a Kennedy [long pause] that got you out of class."

Whenever questioned about his wealth, he used a quip borrowed from Jack: "I have a message from my father —

It often takes two men to keep RFK from being pulled into the crowd.

The family participates in the campaign. Ethel Kennedy with sons (left to right) Chris, Max, and Michael.

'I don't mind spending money, but please don't buy a vote more than is absolutely necessary.'"

In Elkhart, Indiana, he asked the audience, "Will you vote for me?" Audience: "Yeah." "Will you get your friends to vote for me?" Audience: "Yeah." "When people say something bad about me, will you say it isn't true?" Audience: "Yeah." "Have you read my book?" Audience: "Yeah." Kennedy: "You lie."

In Omaha, preceding Vice President Humphrey as a speaker at a Jefferson-Jackson Day banquet, he said, "You have put me ahead of Vice President Humphrey, something I haven't been able to achieve in six weeks of campaigning."

In Brookings, South Dakota, he evoked groans when he referred to "the college." "University?" Cheers. "I can't know everything." More cheers. When the microphone went dead briefly as Kennedy spoke, he tapped it and it came alive: "You just missed my entire farm program."

To a crying baby: "Are you competing with me?" Then, as the crying continued: "Shhh." As the mother rose to take the child out: "Please don't leave. People will say that I'm ruthless."

In Kansas, to a critical questioner who started by saying, "Putting yourself in the president's place. . . ," Kennedy jumped in: "I'm trying to do just that."

When Humphrey got into the race, after Johnson dropped out, Bobby again joked about his own reputation: "I think it was opportunistic of him to come into the race so late. In fact, I think he's very ruthless."

At several stops, he quipped about having been ill and missing several days of work in the Senate. His colleagues had passed a resolution hoping he would get well soon. "The vote was forty-three to forty."

A boy asks a question, and RFK answers in his own way.

In the spotlight, at dusk, on the main street
of a small Indiana town.

60

Prior to entering the race, he denied speculation that he had designs on the White House, and "neither does my wife, Ethelbird."

Occasionally the bantering fell flat. Once a student got up and accused Kennedy of "fifteen minutes of jokes and twenty minutes of double-talk." But, more often, the humor softened the image of Robert Kennedy as opportunistic and pitiless. Many a voter, arriving with a sneer, left with a smile and even, on occasion, a hearty laugh.

The Oregon Trail

By late May of 1968, a nation still sharply divided was nearing the end of the brief primary election season. Robert Kennedy's fundamental situation had not changed. He had won primaries in Indiana, Nebraska, and the District of Columbia. In Alabama and Tennessee and Georgia he had spoken out against racial prejudice. He had gone into urban neighborhoods like Harlem and Watts and Bedford-Stuyvesant, living up to his reputation for "telling it like it is" by urging black audiences to look to their own communities for solutions to their poverty and misery: "You're going to have to do this for yourselves." On college campuses everywhere, he had questioned the student draft deferments, which allowed some to avoid military service while poor whites and blacks and Hispanics who could not afford to go to college were being shipped off to fight in Vietnam. Repeatedly, he had insisted that protests in America be nonviolent — whether against the war, against racial injustice, or against poverty — and that "law and order" be maintained.

Lyndon Johnson had been toppled, but the antiwar vote was still divided between McCarthy and Kennedy. The ever-subservient Hubert Humphrey had been handed Johnson's torch, and the boss-controlled convention delegates would protect the flame unless and until there was clear evidence that Bobby Kennedy could win the election for the Democrats.

Indiana had supplied the first substantive hint of that. It was the first test, outside the New York Senate race, of whether the public excitement for Bobby would transfer into votes. The Democratic bosses insisted that his popularity was as ephemeral as that of a rock star. Kennedy's "new politics," they believed, was a fad indulged by the young — mainly the bearded and beaded — who would not show up at the polls on election day. The "old politics" of labor-union telephone banks and precinct captains getting out the vote would work for Hubert Humphrey, as it had for Lyndon Johnson, and Bobby Kennedy would learn his lesson and get in line for a future nomination.

In Indiana's primary, Kennedy faced McCarthy and the favorite to win this race, the state's Democratic governor, Roger Branigin. The Indianapolis newspapers, owned by far-right publisher Eugene Pulliam, practiced the "old journalism" trick of picking a favorite candidate and playing him up while virtually ignoring his opponents. Kennedy and McCarthy were fortunate to get a mention on the back page, whereas the page-one banner was reserved for stories favorable to Branigin. The governor was not a serious presidential candidate but a stand-in for Johnson and, after the president's departure, for Humphrey. But Pulliam was as anxious as most right-wing Republicans were to see Kennedy and his liberal policies blocked, and Indiana was as good a place as any for that. Pulliam's papers carried one front-page story suggesting that Branigin would be Humphrey's choice for

vice president — a ridiculous notion, since both were mid-westerners and Branigin had no national reputation whatsoever. On primary day, the banner headline read, "Branigin Predicts Sweeping Victory Today."

Despite all the efforts of Pulliam and the Branigin Democratic organization, Robert Kennedy won in Indiana, with Branigin finishing second. McCarthy came in third, but he claimed "victory" because Bobby had been held to under 50 percent of the vote. Although the margin was short of most predictions, it was the character of Kennedy's victory that captured the attention of the party bosses: he carried ten of the eleven congressional districts, all but two cities, ten farm counties, 85 percent of the black vote, and the state's seven largest counties — counties that had been won by George Wallace in 1964 and in which blue-collar workers were the largest voting bloc. To add spice to his triumph and rub a little salt on Eugene Pulliam's wounds, Bobby captured Branigin's home county, his home city, and even his home precinct. "I'll sleep well tonight," he told reporters, "knowing that Eugene Pulliam won't." (Pulliam's grandson, Dan Quayle, became vice president twenty-one years later.)

An elated Fred Dutton tried to put the Indiana victory in perspective: "We need to continue to dramatize the issues. We need to build up momentum. Right now, I doubt if the pros will be overly impressed by our vote percentage [42] in Indiana. But what will begin to sink in on them is that Kennedy is the only candidate who can put the backlash and Negro votes together."

How had he managed to win the support of such disparate and even warring voter blocs? An embittered Eugene McCarthy explained, "By talking out of both sides of his mouth."

Watching Indiana primary returns (left to right): diplomat John Bartlow Martin, Joe Mohbat of the Associated Press, Ethel, Bobby, and Pierre Salinger in Indiana hotel suite.

Analysts, however, noted Kennedy's consistent message in his speeches in black ghettos: "Violence isn't the answer. Violence won't get you better housing or better jobs or better education for your children. The way to change things is by voting for change."

Campaigning among largely white working-class audiences, who had voted for George Wallace four years earlier, Kennedy nearly always used this litany: "The things that cause poverty, the things which lead to rioting and violence, are the things we have to cure." He would also tell blue-collar whites the following, which was, of course, what they wanted to hear: "I believe in law enforcement. I was chief law-enforcement officer of the United States for three and a half years. This nation must have law and order, and if I am elected president of the United States, that is what I intend to see that we have." It would have been out of character for this former attorney general, onetime congressional committee prosecutor, and relentless pursuer of Jimmy Hoffa to fail to make clear his intolerance for lawbreakers. It would, of course, have been poor politics as well.

The momentum of Kennedy's campaign continued, with a big victory in Nebraska and an easy win in the District of Columbia. Next came Oregon.

To this point in the campaign, Bobby Kennedy had won all three primaries he had entered. But he had defeated only McCarthy, by substantial though not overwhelming margins, and, in Indiana, Humphrey surrogate Branigin. These wins were not impressive enough to swing large state delegations to his side. Hubert Humphrey himself campaigned mainly before organized-labor gatherings in big union states such as New Jersey and Michigan, and, fearing Johnson's wrath and the loss of his support, hewed closely to administration policy on the war. On the few occasions when he ventured near college campuses, Humphrey was drowned out by chants of "Dump the Hump" as he vainly tried to defend Johnson on Vietnam.

Unfortunately for Kennedy, relatively few states held direct primaries in 1968. And most of those that did, such as New Hampshire, Indiana, Nebraska, Oregon, and South Dakota, were small, with only a handful of convention delegates to give to the winner. Oregon, with few definable voter blocs, offered Robert Kennedy a last chance to impress party bosses with the breadth of his support. There was only one really big primary, scheduled for June 4 — California.

In the Golden State, where the crowds would be enormous, thanks to Kennedy's "star quality" and to the support of Jesse ("Big Daddy") Unruh, Speaker of the State Assembly and the most powerful politician in his corner, Kennedy could be expected to do well. South Dakota, which Senator George McGovern had pretty well under control — and where Kennedy had campaigned on Indian reservations — looked like a sure thing.

But what if Kennedy came to California on the heels of a loss to McCarthy in Oregon? It was a vision that haunted Bobby and his staff. Oregon was by no means Kennedy country. On a preprimary visit to Salem, the capital, both of its newspapers treated him like a county clerk. One carried no mention of his scheduled appearance; the other published a single sentence at the end of a story on his other stops in Oregon. Only good advance work and word-of-mouth advertising spared the campaign from a major embarrassment. As it turned out, RFK's speech was delivered to a huge crowd on an outdoor plaza in front of the Marion County courthouse.

In addition to press indifference, the Oregon campaign did not allow Kennedy his best hour for other reasons. He hit the state after ten weeks of frenetic campaigning in other states and was bone weary. That affected his performances, of course; audiences found him listless. Yet he had never been received so coolly as he was in Oregon, and that both bothered and puzzled him. Minorities and the underprivileged were too sparsely represented to help the Kennedy cause. There were colleges aplenty, and Kennedy spoke on several campuses. But the cool and cerebral Eugene McCarthy had already appeared on most of them while Kennedy was canvassing the rest of the West Coast and the Midwest. Oregon was too white, too educated, too prosperous for the type of appeal that had spelled victory for Kennedy elsewhere.

At 2:20 on the morning of the Oregon primary, Kennedy was in Los Angeles, waiting for an elevator in the decaying Ambassador Hotel. With him were Freckles, his Irish spaniel, and the itinerant speech writer Dick Goodwin, whose previous experience with McCarthy had led him to predict growing support for that candidacy in Oregon.

Arriving at the hotel after a late flight, covering the campaign for *Time*, I unexpectedly bumped into the small delegation. "How do you feel about Oregon?" I asked the obviously depressed candidate.

Replied Kennedy, "That's the trouble. I just don't know what to feel about Oregon. The people don't really cheer

Sister-in-law Joan Kennedy, delighted by Indiana primary success.

67

Skeptical reporter in hotel ballroom,
Indianapolis, on primary victory night.

you. Sometimes I wish they'd boo me or kick me or do something. I just couldn't get much response."

"Why?"

"I wish I knew. It just wasn't like Indiana and Nebraska." Later that day, he would expand: "I just don't feel as if I ever got a handle on Oregon. I would be happy to win it by one vote. I just want to stay alive."

The campaign that had started as a crusade to end the war, extend opportunity to the underprivileged, advance racial justice, and achieve brotherhood in America, to provide health care to those who could not afford it and "do better" in America, was now in danger of collapsing. The banner retrieved from a fallen president was slipping from Bobby's grasp. "I just want to stay alive," he had said. Millions of Americans wanted their hopes and aspirations to stay alive, too. But this chance would be denied if Robert Kennedy, rejected by the Democrats of Oregon, should then falter in California, a "must" primary for the candidate.

Could Oregon, where Eugene McCarthy's calm, dispassionate intelligence had been so appealing, set a pattern for the rest of the country? Would Oregon awaken Kennedy's America to the likelihood that it was living out a fantasy?

Politicians like Fred Dutton thought Kennedy could survive a narrow loss in Oregon. But if the lost momentum cost him California as well, then it was all over. The Democratic bosses, rid at last of this pest who would impose himself on them, would move on contentedly to nominate Hubert Humphrey, a good and decent soul who was one of their own—someone they could trust to uphold the status quo.

Bobby was still in Los Angeles when word came that, for the first time in twenty-eight political campaigns, one of the three Kennedy brothers had lost. Bobby looked dazed,

Roger Mudd, television news reporter, waits for the senator to speak that night.

69

Bill Barry leads Ethel Kennedy through the celebratory crowd in the ballroom of the Sheraton Lincoln Hotel in downtown Indianapolis.

Delight in the Indiana primary victory is evident.

Disappointed campaign workers watch RFK
concede defeat in the Oregon primary.

baffled. How could a Kennedy, who knew how campaigns were won, lose? He wasn't one to rationalize. When aides told him that his loss was only in network projections, and might not hold up, he was dismissive. "They're usually right," he shrugged.

Given the intensity of this man's desire to become president, and given the depth of his commitment to world peace and to a unified nation, he must have suffered acutely over this setback. Yet outwardly he was unemotional and, though drained, realistic.

"I sometimes wonder," said Robert Kennedy, "if I have correctly sensed the mood of America. I think I have. But maybe I'm all wrong. Maybe the people don't want things changed."

Talking to reporters on his flight back to Portland, he added, "I did my best in Oregon. I think I did everything I could, and the people didn't accept it. But I'm not going to change strategy now. No. I have a program that I believe in and I'm going to continue to press forward with it."

He would not offer excuses, he said. "I lost. When you come in second or third, you lose."

Then he grew pensive again. "I may have misjudged the mood of America," he repeated. "But I still don't think so."

But it was the mood of the convention delegates that was of the most immediate concern. "Well," Kennedy conceded, "I think many of the delegates would seize upon any excuse not to vote for me. Now they have one because I didn't win in Oregon." While agreeing that one of his mistakes in Oregon was underestimating McCarthy, he still gave his foe little or no chance to win the nomination. Even so, he was pained at the intensity of McCarthy's dislike for him. "I think he hates me so much he'd rather stop me than . . ." He did not finish the thought.

He sat silent for a moment. Then he spoke of America's vital need to reconcile the races. Someone boldly asked, "If you don't make it, Bob, who has enough rapport with the poor, the Negroes, and the other minorities" who had so strongly supported him? Always blunt in response to bald questions, Bobby Kennedy declared, "I don't think either one of them has it." Then, reflecting, he agreed that Hubert Humphrey had accomplished much, including the 1948 Democratic platform declaration in behalf of civil rights.

A loss in California would be catastrophic, of course, but he hadn't lost California yet. If he could just put together a victory there, then he could go on as he had planned before — campaigning in nonprimary states as if they were holding primaries, trying to convince the state parties that his popular support was the only hope the Democrats had of retaining control in Washington. With public displays of support and private arm-twisting, he might peel off delegates who preferred Humphrey to Kennedy but who preferred a winner most of all. Such a strategy had made sense for Kennedy before the Oregon loss; he could have gone to the delegates, noting that he had won all six primaries he had entered, that Humphrey had been unwilling to enter any, that as Johnson's vice president Humphrey would take the unpopularity of the incumbent into the general election and would probably lose, whereas Kennedy, with no such burden, just might win. But had Oregon, and its possible carryover to California, ruined all that? If so, it had ruined the Robert Kennedy crusade. Without a solid win in California, he would have to bring his candidacy to an end.

Only Larry O'Brien's optimistic voice pierced the gloom. A key tactician who had played a crucial role in all of John F. Kennedy's victories, O'Brien was unshaken. "Of course we took a beating," he sniffed. "There aren't many pluses

A dispirited RFK and entourage leave Oregon
the next morning en route to Los Angeles.

Bobby and speech writer Dick Goodwin
in a state of semishock on the plane.

Consoling words from writer Theodore H. White aboard the plane.

76

in losing. But there could be a hidden one here." Bobby Kennedy had previously had the family aura of invincibility. Like his brothers, if he couldn't win an election fair and square, it was widely held that he could usually buy it. This didn't sit well with the public. Furthermore, O'Brien went on, Bobby added arrogance to his share of that family reputation. Now he was no longer invincible. To some degree, O'Brien theorized, maybe his image had been humanized in defeat. For the first time, a Kennedy of the Jack–Bob–Ted generation had acquired the aura of an underdog.

On to California.

The Crusade in the Crucible

Defeat focuses the mind sharply — particularly when one is accustomed to victory. After the wake-up call in Oregon, Kennedy's managers realized what the Kennedys should have known since Jack's first campaign for Congress in 1946: that politics is a profession, and it requires professionals at the controls. The time for key roles to be played by friendly amateurs was over. In Oregon, Bobby had let his friend Bill vanden Heuvel and one of his few supporters in Congress, Edith Green of Oregon, manage the campaign. They weren't responsible for the loss — the candidate took the blame for that. But now pros like Dutton, O'Brien, Mankiewicz, and Steve Smith — and Robert Kennedy himself — would be in charge.

They would give McCarthy no more free rides. Instead of campaigning as if his opponent did not exist, Kennedy would respond henceforth to every McCarthy charge. The political cognoscenti were aware that the major threat to Kennedy's nomination was Humphrey, but the average voter in Oregon hadn't grasped why Kennedy was targeting the faraway Humphrey when Eugene McCarthy was berating Kennedy on the next street corner. McCarthy had been blaming Bobby for the Bay of Pigs (the abortive attempt to topple Castro), the original major buildup of U.S. forces in Vietnam, and the appointments to John Kennedy's cabinet of Dean Rusk and Robert McNamara, two architects of the failed Vietnam policy. McCarthy also accused Bobby of "coming late" to an antiwar position, a charge that was false (he had spoken out publicly before McCarthy had) but that had resonance with voters, who were aware that Bobby had indeed come late to the campaign. Bobby agreed that he had allowed too many McCarthy criticisms to go unanswered; in fact, he had so badly underestimated McCarthy that he was not even aware of much of what his rival had been saying. The Minnesotan, in turn, charged Kennedy with falsifying the McCarthy record.

One of the campaign's many ironies was McCarthy's television and print advertising that flayed the "Kennedy machine." In Oregon, the machine had not even been in evidence. Vanden Heuvel, a New Yorker, knew little about the state, and Edith Green was ineffective. Steve Smith and Ted Kennedy spent hardly any time in the state, and Larry O'Brien hadn't been able to get there until after the Nebraska primary. Frank Mankiewicz had stayed in California to shore up the organization for that key state primary. In essence, no one had been in charge of the Robert Kennedy campaign in Oregon. Although McCarthy painted vivid pictures of a Kennedy juggernaut spewing cash in every corner of the

Young man in the crowd
in California, 1968.

state, the McCarthy campaign actually spent more money in Oregon than did Kennedy, who was saving funds for an all-out effort in California.

Bobby hadn't helped matters at all. Before the polls opened, he had publicly conceded that if he lost in Oregon "I would not be a very viable candidate for president." The comment reaped a harvest of unwelcome newspaper headlines and negative broadcast reports. He compounded this gaffe after the loss by commenting that California had a "more representative" voting population and he therefore would abide by the decision of the voters there. The California papers had a field day, with headlines such as "Bobby to Quit — If" in the *Los Angeles Herald Examiner*. The candor that endeared Robert Kennedy to his loyalists was crippling his campaign.

Probably the most damaging mistake had been Bobby's refusal to debate McCarthy. Although a common tactic for candidates who are far better known than their opponents, such a refusal frequently leads to embarrassing incidents — as it did in Oregon. Everywhere there were signs in the "What Are You Afraid of, Bobby?" genre, but the real damage occurred when the two campaigns happened to cross paths. Bobby, not wanting to be confronted by McCarthy when television cameras were grinding, disappeared. Genially, McCarthy pretended to be looking for Bobby, but actually he headed straight for the Kennedy press bus and scornfully bewailed his opponent's "cowardice." Television and newspaper coverage was unsparing.

Despite such a damaging experience, Kennedy advisers argued against a debate in California after the polls showed a substantial Kennedy lead. Why risk it? McCarthy — well

Bobby had drawn mixed, sometimes ominous reactions
from crowds in Los Angeles in 1966.

over six feet tall, movie-star handsome (he reminded many people of actor Ray Milland), and polished—might come off much better on television than the shorter, frequently rumpled, "hotter" Kennedy. In the end, it was the candidate himself who made the risky decision to debate, and for a very Bobby-like reason. "He couldn't stand those shouts of 'coward' in Oregon," explained Fred Dutton.

The campaign, on the morning after the Oregon loss, had clearly undergone a major transformation. It was now all business, no nonsense. So swiftly did the retinue vacate Portland's Benson Hotel that some members of the entourage were left behind and had to make their own way to Los Angeles, the next stop. There the police, with encouragement from the anti-Kennedy mayor, Sam Yorty, gave out hundreds of traffic tickets to the Kennedy motorcade.

The crowds in Los Angeles were enormous. Advance men and Jesse Unruh had done their work well, and voter interest may have been piqued by the first Kennedy loss in an election. The size and warmth of the crowds got the Kennedy juices flowing again. But all was not well. At a rally at Los Angeles International Airport, Bobby grimaced at a sign asking, "Does Bobby Have Oregonic Fever?" When his eyes fell on another sign, which said, "Oregon—Sorry About That," he quipped, "So am I."

To those who had been on the campaign from day one, it was clear that the candidate was a bit more hesitant, a little less confident, a lot more inclined to stammer—evidence enough that he had been severely shaken by what had happened to him in Oregon. Still, as he gazed out at the enthusiastic crowds, he could not help feeling more "at home" than he had in weeks. This was an electorate he could deal with. Blacks, Hispanic-Americans, farm workers, the poor,

Jews, and plenty of Catholics contrasted with the nearly all-white, overwhelmingly Protestant gatherings in Oregon.

Although reluctant to give renewed life to the old "Ruthless Robert" image, Kennedy nonetheless felt that he had to respond to McCarthy's accusations. If Oregon was a guide, the cost of not answering would be more damaging than the specter of the "bad Bobby" resurrected. Thus, in San Bernardino, he served up an example of the new strategy. When McCarthy supporters yelled, "You're late," as Bobby launched into a discussion of how to end the war in Vietnam, he snarled, "Of all the candidates for president, I was the first one to speak out against the way that war was being fought. Don't ask me why Gene McCarthy voted for the Gulf of Tonkin resolution." (By way of this infamous ruse, Lyndon Johnson had won congressional authority to respond to an attack on U.S. ships by the North Vietnamese. The attack never occurred.) In Oregon, McCarthy had boasted of being one of five senators, not including Robert Kennedy, who had later voted to rescind the resolution. But Kennedy's harsh attack on McCarthy fell largely on deaf ears. Few of his San Bernardino listeners had any notion of what the Gulf of Tonkin resolution was.

The great debate in San Francisco was next. It would be televised nationally, but the immediate impact on California voters would be its most crucial outcome. There is no more risky venture in politics than a debate. Rarely do voters fixate on what the candidates say. A day later, in the absence of a memorable zinger, the stances on the issues are largely forgotten. What sticks is an impression of the debaters, of the kind of people they appear to be. Most often, minds have already been made up, but candidates are aware that if they appear hesitant or lose their cool they will pay a heavy price at the polls. The feeling in the Kennedy camp was that Bobby had little to gain and much to lose in a confrontation with the smooth and articulate McCarthy. But McCarthy had made it impossible for his rival to refuse. Jesse Unruh had reported that 75 percent to 80 percent of McCarthy's advertising in California would trumpet Kennedy's "cowardice" in the face of his debate challenge.

There was no shortage of intellectual firepower in San Francisco to help the candidate prepare. Arthur Schlesinger and writer-diplomat John Bartlow Martin joined Ted Sorensen, Dick Goodwin, Dutton, and political hands Steve Smith and Ted Kennedy for long hours in the candidate's suite in San Francisco, not simply tutoring him on the issues but trying to anticipate the ways in which McCarthy would try to trip him up. Actually, Bobby needed only to memorize the dates of his antiwar speeches and statements; he was certain that McCarthy would press the "latecomer" charge. In Washington, the campaign staff was compiling a dossier of McCarthy speeches, with the focus on the dates they were delivered.

In one sense, the debate offered Kennedy a valuable opportunity to be seen, as McCarthy invariably was, in a calm studio rather than on a street corner, on a campus, or in a shopping mall, his hair blowing in the wind, people shouting and groping. "I'm seen too often as the 'frenetic' candidate," he complained, whereas McCarthy generally appeared seated in a serene and orderly setting, with a newsman asking him questions.

Before the cameras started rolling, Kennedy and McCarthy insisted on some ground rules. Questions would be confined to issues. Neither wanted to be asked where his support would go if he were to lose the primary. Both

Campaigning in Watts,
RFK has no police protection,
relying instead on a group
called the "Sons of Watts."

Bodyguard Bill Barry's birthday becomes the highlight of one long trip through California. Here, Ethel and Dick Tuck bring the cake down the aisle of the plane.

Bobby and reporters laughing with Barry. (On Bobby's right, Richard Harwood of the *Washington Post*, and on his left, Joe Mohbat of the Associated Press.)

wanted a near-empty studio, with only close friends and top aides present; and each side would choose one correspondent for a two-person "pool." Facilities were provided on the fourth floor for other reporters, who would view the proceedings on television monitors. Bobby, Ethel, and their small party arrived at the studio on that Saturday, June 1, pulling up to an empty curbside. McCarthy, who was said to have "drilled" for the debate by playing catch with an aide in his hotel room, was greeted by a swarm of volunteers. Both candidates were aware of the most recent polls, which showed Kennedy ahead. Thus, if Kennedy could avoid a major blunder, his agreeing to debate would prove to have been a wise move.

Like so many encounters involving presidential candidates, the San Francisco face-off of Robert Kennedy and Eugene McCarthy produced very little excitement. Kennedy accused his rival of "distorting" his record in McCarthy's Oregon advertisements, and McCarthy was his usual witty, charming, laid-back self. Each accused the other of distorting his Senate voting record. As expected, Bobby was more intense, and he committed what afterward would be regarded as a minor gaffe. When McCarthy spoke vaguely about an idea he had previously floated — moving people out of the ghettos and into the suburbs — Kennedy commented on the disruptive impact of ten thousand Negroes transplanted to public housing in Orange County, California's main bastion of conservatism. McCarthy paid little attention to this slight to blacks until the following day. But the Kennedy support in the black community was so unshakable that the flap was soon forgotten.

After the debate, the Kennedy crusade was held to be solidly on track. Kennedy's performance had been no better than McCarthy's, but it had been no worse, either. And when you are the front-runner all you need to do is hold your own. Three days later, on Tuesday, June 4, Californians would go to the polls. Bobby Kennedy was confident. The debate, his pollsters had told him, was his last major hurdle. Once safely past that, he would go on to win that race.

On the flight back to Los Angeles, the candidate was elated and, as always, candid. Would he win California? I asked.

"Yes," said Bobby.

But it would take a massive effort after that to stop Hubert Humphrey, who had the bosses and big labor in his corner. Kennedy spoke of "a coalition of some sort." Although he did not elaborate, a coalition could only involve McCarthy; after losing to Kennedy in California, McCarthy would surely sense that the cause for which he and Kennedy had entered the race was bigger than both of them and that the only way to advance it now was to forge an alliance between the peace candidates. Humphrey would be obliged to defend Johnson's record and policies, and he would lose to Nixon, whose willingness to pursue peace was even more suspect.

But if there were no coalition, if Humphrey were to win the nomination?

"I would support Humphrey," said Bobby. "I don't know if I would campaign for him." Presumably that would demand some softening of Humphrey's stand on the war.

"Hubert has lost touch." Bobby thought that McCarthy's legions of young voters would certainly prefer himself to Johnson's vice president and that many would switch to him after California, despite their bitterness over McCarthy's demise. "It just depends upon how many."

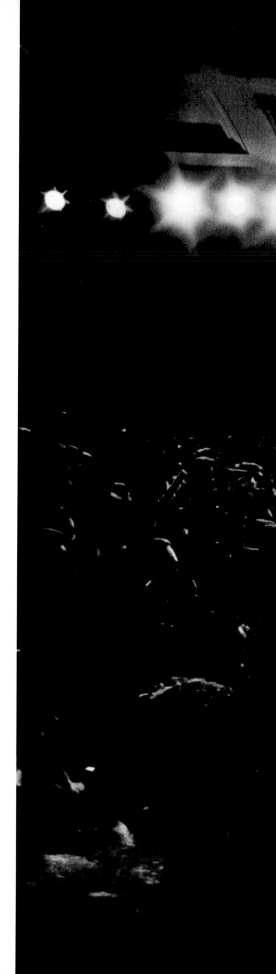

Bobby and Ethel face a jubilant crowd in the ballroom of the Ambassador Hotel after his victory in the California primary, June 4, 1968.

THE AMBASSADOR HOTEL

"This Way, Senator"

Tuesday, June 4, 1968, in Los Angeles was a day of inexplicable foreboding. The leaden sky joined forces with the smog to blot out even the notion of a sun. The air was heavy and oppressive, slowing down everything that moved, including, it seemed, the hands of clocks.

The Kennedy entourage wanted to enjoy this day but couldn't. The political operatives were glued to their telephones; everyone else had the day off. Even so, the swimming pool at the Ambassador Hotel was deserted. The candidate, his wife, and six of their children were gone for the day, staying at a luxurious home on the beach at Malibu. The press, always jittery when the object of its labors is out of sight, chafed, but the reporters were too tired to lodge a serious complaint.

Bobby's absence certainly accounted for some of the day's unease. Only the day

Upstairs in RFK's suite earlier in the evening, friends and family watch election returns on TV.

before, as the Kennedy motorcade had snaked through San Francisco's Chinatown, Ethel had lurched forward at the staccato sound of firecrackers, her arms clutching her chest, her eyes filled with terror. The Kennedy aides — those who had been in Dallas and those who had suffered through it vicariously — momentarily stiffened, then gratefully shed their anxiety as the candidate continued to grab and be grabbed by the adoring throngs.

After the debate in San Francisco, there had been visits to Watts and then Compton. Hands — white and black, young and old — reached out to touch this rich easterner with the magical allure. He wouldn't stop campaigning until late on the eve of the primary. Then, even after most of his staff and many of the traveling press had dropped out, exhausted, Bobby Kennedy took his cause on to San Diego. On this night before the California primary, supporters had gathered at a San Diego motel. Bone weary, the candidate completed one speech, then abruptly sat down and held his head in his hands. Pale and unsteady, he half walked and was half carried to a men's room by the ever-faithful Bill Barry, Rafer Johnson, and Roosevelt Grier. After vomiting, he returned to the podium and briefly addressed a new audience, closing the speech with his trademark signal to reporters that it was time for them to head for the press bus: "As George Bernard Shaw said, 'Some men see things as they are and say why; I dream things that never were and ask why not?'" For eleven weeks, often a dozen or more times a day, they had heard Bobby Kennedy thus paraphrase Shaw. They could not know that they would not hear those familiar words from him again.

On the thirty-five-minute return flight to Los Angeles, the candidate slept, insisting that he felt "fine." Too anxious to rest, Ethel took a center seat between two of the traveling

Above: Michael and Kerry Kennedy
(in foreground), with David Hackett
and Jean Kennedy Smith behind
them; top left: Jeff Greenfield (in
foreground); bottom left: John
Bartlow Martin.

With two primary victories assured, Bobby gives a few high-spirited interviews before heading toward the ballroom. (Hays Gorey is second from left, top photo.)

On the way through the kitchen to the ballroom, RFK
signs a rolled-up poster for a campaign volunteer.

He shakes the hand of a shy kitchen helper.

correspondents. She was well aware of what was at stake — a defeat in the California primary would be more than a lost election. It would mean that Bobby Kennedy's promises to seek peace, to try to curb racism, to find ways to lift up the downtrodden would be put on hold. Nervously, Ethel asked, "What do you think will happen tomorrow?" Relax, said Dick Harwood of the *Washington Post*; Bobby will win. Skeptical, as most political wives learn to be, she replied, "I know you think so. But you see so many of the crowds and the people who love him. You don't hear the others."

"The others" — out there were plenty of "others," who knew, to their consternation, that Bobby would try to keep his campaign pledges and might succeed.

After a few hours of sleep, the reporters conveyed to one another their distaste for election days. They had become accustomed to the frenetic dawn-to-dusk electioneering, and suddenly there was little for anyone to do. Larry O'Brien, the joyful Irish pol with the deep voice and the ready laugh, tried to elevate their spirits. O'Brien was totally upbeat. "This could be quite a day, quite a day," he mused, with annoying good cheer. "Two hundred Democratic delegates in one day — California and South Dakota. A red-letter day. And next we'll have Bobby hit the bricks in New York. More delegates, and . . ." His voice trailed off. The most professional and probably the most honest of all the politicians traveling with Kennedy, O'Brien felt obliged to add, "The nomination is within our grasp. But it's not locked up."

At nightfall, to everyone's relief, the candidate and his family returned safely to the Ambassador from Malibu. Fred Dutton, the only aide who had accompanied them, told reporters a chilling story: twelve-year-old David Kennedy, caught in an undertow, had been rescued by his father, who dove after him. Dutton likely would have said nothing, but reporters noticed a cut near the candidate's eye and demanded to know what had happened. The incident was "nothing," Bobby insisted, fearful that reports of his "heroism" would simply fuel suspicions that the Kennedys would do anything — even stage a near-drowning — in order to win an election.

In the Kennedy suite, as the returns slowly trickled in, the candidate was in a remarkably mellow mood. A few reporters and cameramen were admitted to the rooms to mingle with staff, hangers-on, and an assortment of Kennedys, including daughters Kerry and Courtney and sons David and Michael. For a change, Kennedy was not tense. He was satisfied, he declared, with his life in politics, and he quoted Lord Tweedsmuir to the effect that politics is an "honorable adventure." The returns from South Dakota indicated an overwhelming victory, and early projections of the California vote had Kennedy beating McCarthy. The Golden State wasn't Oregon. California had blocs to which Kennedy had a particular appeal. His confidence contrasted with the discouraged mood of the week before.

"What's next?" someone asked.

"We'll go to New York Thursday or Friday," said Kennedy. "First we'll be meeting here with all our people." Then he excused himself, caught an encouraging bulletin on television, and huddled with Dutton, Dick Drayne (Ted Kennedy's press secretary), and Dick Goodwin.

"Hey, Bobby," someone called out. "Is it too early to say congratulations?"

The victory speech in the ballroom.

The reply: "Yes—unless you mean South Dakota."

"Is McCarthy becoming more of a politician than a crusader?" asked a headline-hungry journalist. The candidate refused the bait. "I like politicians. I don't consider distorting the record politics."

"What would you call it?" Bobby's silence meant that no "Kennedy Flays McCarthy" headline the next morning would compete with the one already being envisioned: "Kennedy Wins California Primary."

"What will you do after the election?"

"Have a drink. Maybe three."

Wearing their longest faces, Adam Walinsky, aide Milt Gwirtzman, Ted Sorensen, and Dick Goodwin entered the suite, all obviously under strict orders not to convey an optimism that might not hold up throughout the evening. Ethel, with her children and friends Blanche Whittaker and Susan Markham, fended off attempts by reporters to trap them into premature declarations of victory. Comedian Pat Paulsen appeared on the television and gave everyone a chance to laugh, even though Kennedy was now trailing McCarthy in the actual tally—as opposed to the projections, which were wildly optimistic. The candidate was less relaxed than he had been and seemed relieved to forget the vote count for a moment in order to congratulate Los Angeles Dodgers pitcher Don Drysdale via telephone for pitching his fifth consecutive shutout. As 11:30 approached, the networks, losing their audience by the minute (the East, where it was 2:30 A.M., had largely gone to bed), pressured Kennedy to declare victory. The projections showed Kennedy far ahead—even though he actually won by only 140,000 votes out of 3 million cast. In any event, everyone dashed for the elevators, women losing shoes or breaking their heels in the mad rush to reach the ballroom, where the Robert Kennedy campaign would bask in its finest moment.

The candidate, surrounded by photographers and cameramen, strode briskly through the hotel kitchen, pausing briefly for autographs and to greet some of the kitchen help. When he reached the huge, packed ballroom, the heat was stifling, but no one minded. These were true believers, whose beliefs had just been validated. Bobby Kennedy had just won a tremendous victory. Not everyone could hear what he was saying over the crowd's cheering, but they knew its essence. He would press on with fervor, he would fight for every last delegate, and if he won the nomination (and of course he would) he would go on to victory in November. And in the White House he would try to restore what the nation had lost when his older brother was slain. To those in the Ambassador Hotel ballroom on June 4, 1968, and to all who shared their dream, the night was theirs.

When it was time for Robert Kennedy to abandon the podium, someone said, "This way, senator," and the party headed back through the kitchen toward the Colonial Room, where the winner of the California Democratic primary would grant his first postvictory interviews to the reporters who had covered his campaign from the start.

"This way, senator." Soon after, there was a sound, eerily like the noise of the firecrackers the day before in Chinatown.

But it wasn't the same, it wasn't firecrackers, and somehow everyone knew it. Now a kitchen helper supported the felled candidate, whose eyes were vacant, his lithe body limp.

Gunfire in the kitchen. At this point, Bill Eppridge is about twelve feet behind the senator. "I push CBS cameraman Jim Wilson toward the shooting. My camera accidentally goes off."

"We first encounter the prone form of
Paul Schrade, a UAW official, who
has also been shot."

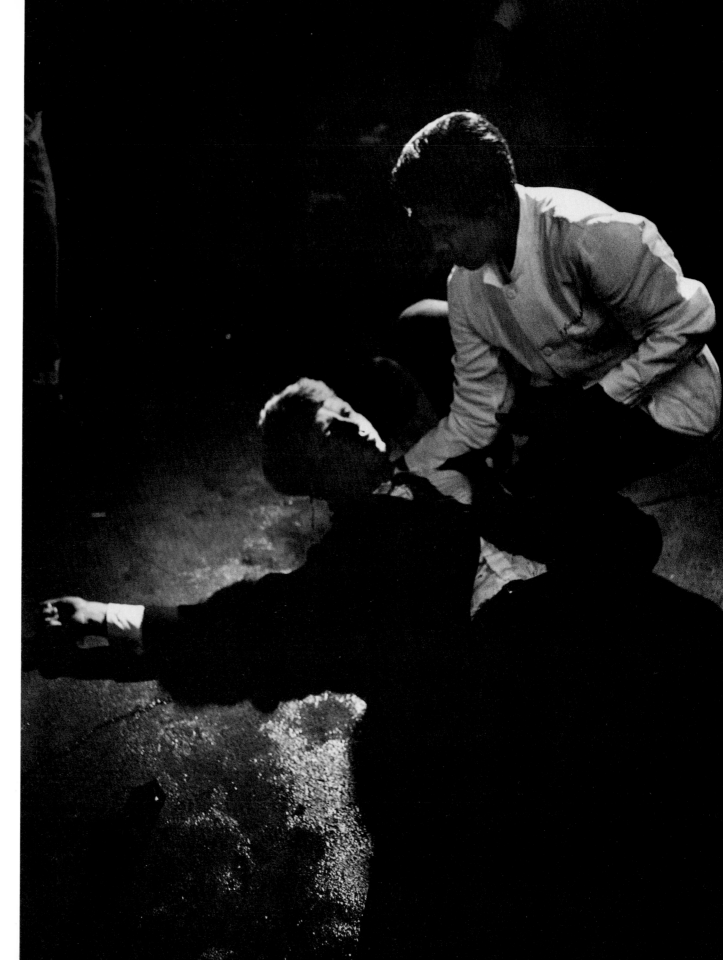

A few feet from Schrade lies Bobby, bleeding from a head wound. Juan Romero, a busboy who had been shaking RFK's hand when Sirhan Sirhan fired the gun, attempts to raise the senator's head.

Romero looks up in anguish, eyes pleading for assistance.

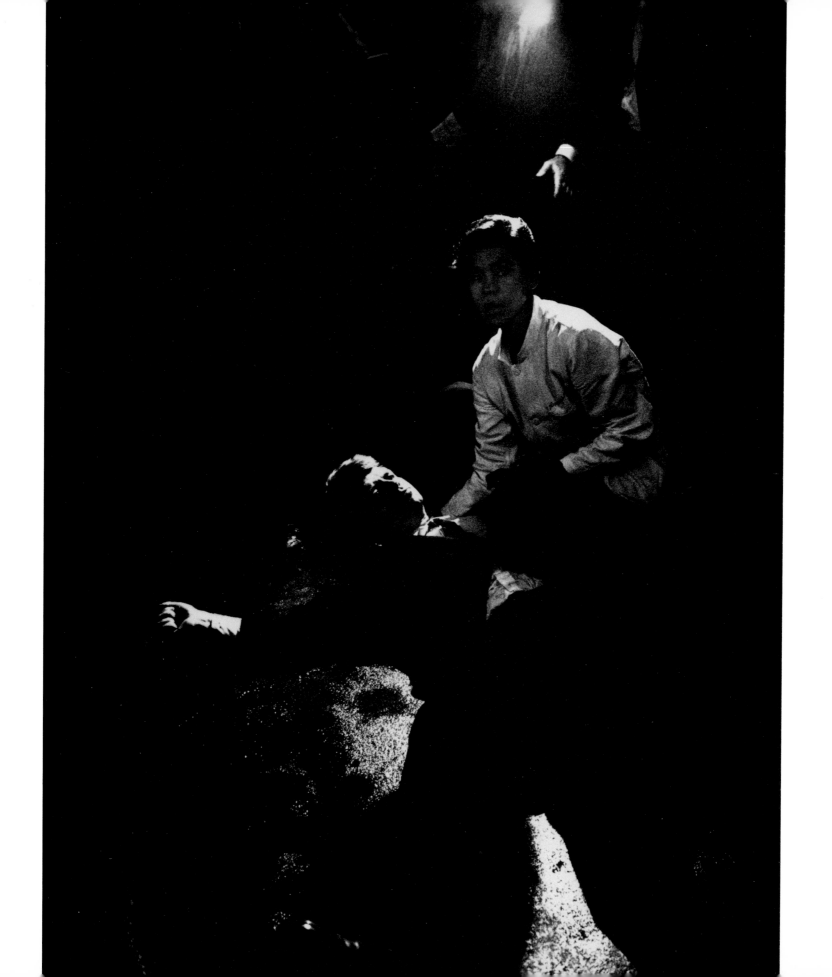

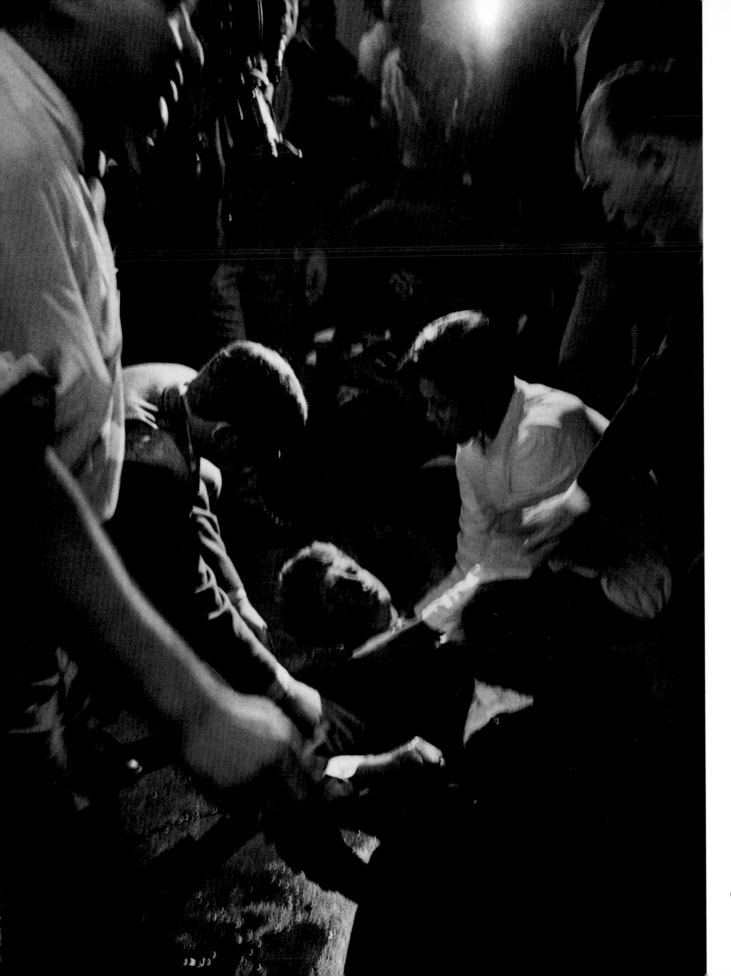

Others rush in to help.

The scene turns to bedlam.

Ethel Kennedy is brought to her husband's side.

Horrified campaign adviser, Fred Dutton.

Ethel tries to clear the room.

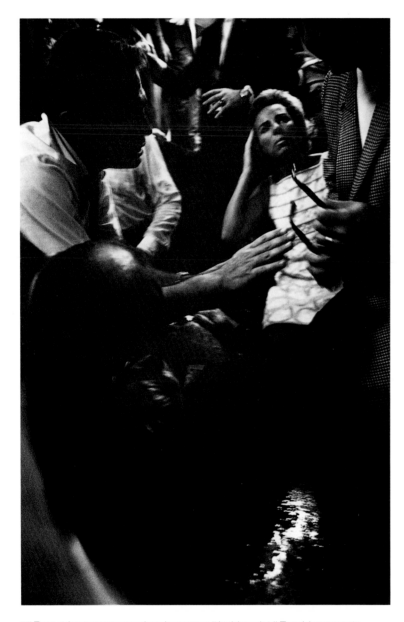

Bill Barry tries to remove a local reporter. "At this point," Eppridge reports, "I feel it is time for me to back away. I move back and put my arms out to restrain the crowd. Once or twice, I reach down to trigger the camera hanging from my neck."

"I Have a Short Announcement to Read"

Pandemonium. Confusion. Horror.

"No, God, it can't be!" cried a female voice. But there lay Bobby Kennedy, sprawled on the cold concrete. Three of his entourage, Jack Gallivan, Jr., George Plimpton, and Bill Barry, struggled with a slight, dark-complexioned gunman, trying in vain to wrest a black pistol from his grasp. They backed him up against a table. A small man vaulted onto the table and stamped on the gunman's right arm and hand, but still he would not let go. Roosevelt Grier and Rafer Johnson, muscular athletes both, took over the captive and pried loose his weapon. Finally, the police arrived.

Bobby Kennedy lay wounded. We in that kitchen realized more than ever how valuable and beloved he was. There was still hope. His eyes were open. He looked at people. Some said his expression was one of resignation, as if to say, "So this is the way it's going to end." But Bobby had always been a fatalist. Reporters used to ask him if he had to motor around in an open convertible, presenting himself as such a tempting target, when so many "crazies" lurked out there, and he would reply that if someone wanted to get him badly enough a way would be found. Meanwhile he would not insulate himself from the people.

Bill Barry, Kennedy's only bodyguard, was shouting, "Hughie, give me your coat! Take off your coat, Hughie!" And Hugh McDonald, only twenty-nine, an assistant press secretary, complied, although he seemed dazed. All evening, McDonald had posted himself at the entrance to the sweltering Embassy Room, checking credentials for the security officers and barring anyone without the proper tags. Now

One of the frames shot from the hip. Ethel speaks to her husband. Jean Smith, his sister, is to the right.

Hugh McDonald had to wonder if he had admitted the gunman who had shot Robert Kennedy. He had not, but he did not yet know that, and the thought was destroying him. Barry had put his own coat under Kennedy's head, and now, using McDonald's coat, he tried to stanch the flow of blood from a wound above the senator's right ear.

"Get back, get back, everybody — let the senator have some air," Barry screamed. An eternity, it seemed, passed before a doctor, a paramedic, an ambulance driver, some-one — anyone — with even a smidgen of medical knowledge arrived. Behind Kennedy, another man lay sprawled — Paul Schrade, a California United Auto Workers official. He appeared to be dead, but wasn't.

Bobby's right knee was bent, and he could move it ever so slightly, giving hope. At times his eyes rolled; at others they appeared clear and focused. His breathing was labored, but at least he was breathing — you could see and hear that.

Ethel had lagged behind, greeting friends and thanking Bobby's supporters. As soon as Roger Mudd, the burly CBS correspondent, realized what had happened to Bobby, he found Ethel and formed a one-man wedge to bring her through the crowd.

Kneeling at her husband's side, she whispered to him. You could see his lips move as he spoke to her. A hopeful sign. Ethel stood up, trying to wave people back. Others joined in, and then she fell to her knees again. She was in control, remarkably so. Bill Eppridge tried to hold back the crowd, occasionally taking a picture without bothering to bring his eye to the camera dangling from his neck. Still no doctor appeared.

Frank Mankiewicz buried his head in someone's back,

weeping softly. Jesse Unruh was like a madman. "I want him alive," he shouted to the cops holding the dark-haired gunman. "I want him alive!" Unruh then began to strike out at the photographers who were still trying to shoot pictures of Kennedy.

Hugh McDonald looked toward the serving table. Chaos surrounded the gunman, whose name, it turned out, was Sirhan Sirhan — an Arab unhinged by Kennedy's support for Israel. McDonald (who was later to die of an overdose of medication, unable to shake this dreadful experience) said afterward, "I didn't care whether the guy got away or not. All I cared about was the senator. I thought maybe the wounds weren't serious. He was conscious and rational." The senator's last words, except for those he spoke to Ethel, were: "Is everybody else all right?"

At last doctors arrived. After another eon there was a stretcher. Kennedy's lips were moving. They seemed to say, "Don't. Don't. Don't lift me." But of course he had to be lifted, and finally he was on his way to a hospital.

Reporters, photographers, and staff followed as best they could. Bill Eppridge spotted a cab that a woman had just hired. "Lady, I'll give you fifty dollars if you let me have this cab. Robert Kennedy's been shot, and I've got to get to the hospital." She gave up the cab and refused the fifty dollars. I flagged a passing motorist, told him what had happened. Would the driver take me to the nearest hospital? He would. Five other reporters piled in. John Glenn, with *Life* columnist Loudon Wainright, stopped three cars. None would take them. Wainright shrieked at one driver, "Don't you know who this is? This is John Glenn, the astronaut. He's Senator Kennedy's friend. Now take us to the hospital." Unim-

Reporters wait outside Good Samaritan Hospital.

Press and campaign workers crowd the front entrance of the hospital.

pressed, the driver waved them off. On the fourth try they succeeded.

The ambulance took Robert Kennedy to a small receiving hospital about a mile distant. Journalists massed in the hall until the police pushed them back. Inside, a hospital security guard stopped Ethel as she raced to get to Bobby's side. "But I'm Mrs. Kennedy!" she screamed. "I don't care who you are, lady," he responded, displaying a badge, whereupon she slapped it out of his hand. Fred Dutton and Dick Tuck, the notorious campaign prankster, each grabbed an arm and muscled the guard aside. "I'll get you for assault and battery," the guard cried. "That's all right," Tuck yelled. "My name is Dick Tuck. Get me." John Glenn got inside the hospital and safely past one policeman. But two others stopped him and strong-armed him against a wall. Ted Sorensen and Dick Goodwin, who were reliving the nightmare of Dallas 1963, asked to be admitted and were turned back. After lengthy arguments the police agreed to their plea to send word to the family that they were there. Word came back to admit them to the corridor.

Reporters, not knowing if Kennedy was alive or dead, spied a Catholic priest coming down the hall and beckoned him to come outside. Surprisingly, he complied, looking exceedingly glum until he neared the door and permitted himself a polite smile. He was Father Peacha, he said, and he had been driving near the hospital when he heard a radio report that Robert Kennedy was there. So he had stopped in. Had he administered the last rites? He had. But he could shed no light on the senator's condition.

After a long wait, Frank Mankiewicz appeared, escorted by a policeman. The press secretary was surprisingly upbeat. Senator Kennedy had two bullet wounds in the head,

One of Eugene McCarthy's campaign workers at the hospital.

A local reporter shows mug shots of Sirhan Sirhan to police outside the hospital.

Press secretary Frank Mankiewicz
at a press conference outside the
hospital, pointing to the place where
the fatal bullet hit RFK.

Mankiewicz said. His condition was "stable." He was breathing well. "He has a good heart." And he was being transferred to the Hospital of the Good Samaritan. The newsmen rushed there, but by this time the Los Angeles Police Department was out in force. A dozen officers kept the journalists behind a red rubber mat that was a considerable distance from the main entrance. A handful were able to get inside, among them Bill Eppridge, who, camera concealed and wearing a tie, apparently was mistaken for a doctor or a family member and walked right in.

A crowd gathered. Reporters exchanged rumors and personal responses. One said that someone inside the hospital had walked near the glass entrance doors and signaled to him with a thumbs-up sign. Was he a reliable source? "Of course." Joe Mohbat of the Associated Press said that when he first heard of a shooting he kept repeating to himself, over and over, "It isn't Kennedy. It isn't Kennedy."

Hours later, the senator's press secretary emerged from the hospital to brief the reporters a second time. As Frank Mankiewicz climbed atop an automobile so he could be seen and heard by all, his face, wreathed in anguish, bore the crux of the message: Bobby Kennedy was dead or dying. Mankiewicz appeared to have aged fifteen years since earlier that night. His walk was wooden, and his voice cracked. His eyes were glazed. Somehow, he managed to say that Senator Kennedy was alive, still breathing by himself, in intensive care. One of the bullets, he croaked, was in the brain. "Do you have hope for complete recovery?" someone shouted. Mankiewicz stared, muttered something about everyone being hopeful, patiently fielded other questions. His assistant, Hugh McDonald, emerged from the hospital and wan-

dered, dazed, beyond a police barricade. He was shoved and shouted back by the police, triggering a verbal confrontation with the press, who knew, as the cops apparently did not, that McDonald was out of it. Fred Dutton, totally composed, coatless, tieless, tried in vain to quiet the by now swollen press corps for the sake of the other hospital patients.

Subsequent briefings by Mankiewicz sowed as much confusion as light. Reports that Kennedy's condition was "very critical" and that he was unconscious were interspersed with reports that "life signs are good." Three hours of surgery removed "most" of a bullet lodged near the brain stem, but a fragment remained.

As life slipped away from Robert Kennedy, the people who had chronicled his odyssey in word and picture during every waking moment of the past three months—the press— sank into despair. We found objectivity impossible to maintain for the moment. Skeptics at first, we had seen and heard Robert Kennedy in endless situations where he was undeniably genuine. Under the code of our profession, we couldn't write it or photograph it, but we knew it was true, and now we had to say it—if only to each other. A reporter had kept in his wallet a copy of that paraphrase of Shakespeare that had comforted Bobby when Jack died, and that Bobby had borrowed in Indianapolis the night Martin Luther King, Jr., was slain. The reporter now read the passage aloud: "When he shall die, take him out and cut him into little stars and he shall make the face of heaven so shine that all the world will be in love with night and take no worship from the garish sun."

Throughout the night, Dutton, Goodwin, Tuck, Salinger, John Seigenthaler, Bill Barry, and others tried in vain to

Eppridge manages to walk past security into the hospital, cameras under his coat.

John Glenn and family friend David Hackett talk with police officials.

Bill Barry (in shirt sleeves) with campaign staffers in the hallway
outside Senator Kennedy's room.

Barry walks away, realizing the extent of RFK's wounds.

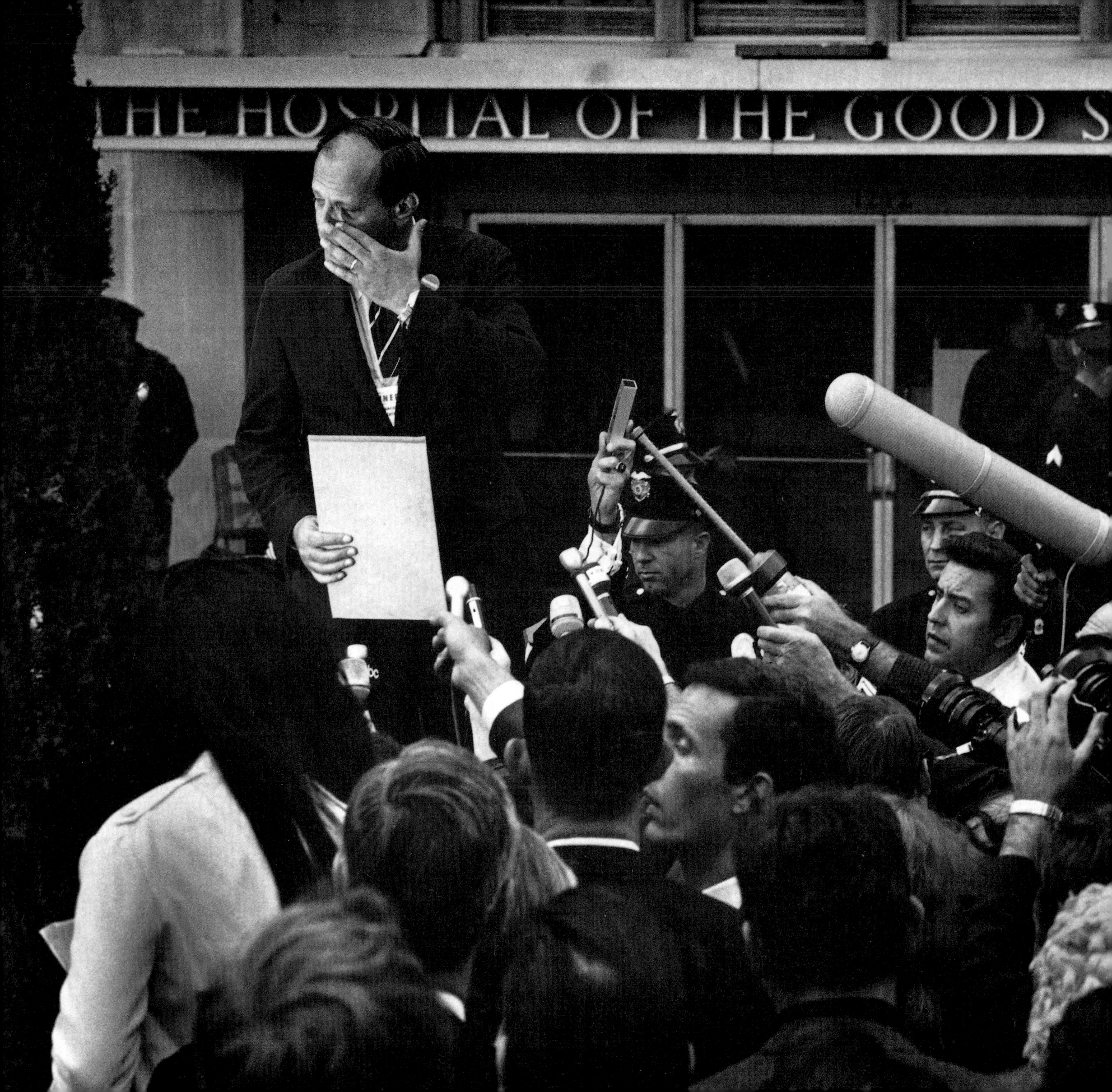
HOSPITAL OF THE GOOD

buoy each other's spirits. Ethel remained at her husband's side. At dawn, the press corps was joined outside the hospital by Los Angeles residents, many wearing "Pray for Bobby" signs on the backs of their jackets or coats.

Night fell again, and, as is always the case when information is scarce, rumors proliferated. Bobby was dead, but word was being held up until Jackie Kennedy could reach the hospital. That report disintegrated when Jackie arrived and nothing was announced. Well, now they were waiting until the rest of the Kennedy children were on hand. No, no — they were holding back until adequate security precautions could be taken in Watts and other black areas. It was midnight, twenty-four hours after the shooting. No one had slept or could sleep. Nor could anyone recall when he or she had last eaten. A new and better rumor took hold — Kennedy was alive. Otherwise, the rest of the children would not have been flown out.

Now it was 2:00 A.M. For the tenth time, the lights of the television cameras came on, this time for a purpose. Frank Mankiewicz emerged. He who had spurned lucrative offers to practice law, who had turned his back on a writing career in Hollywood, where his father and uncle had won fame and fortune, who had instead accepted a low-paying job with Robert Kennedy "because this is where the action is" now stepped to a microphone.

"I have a short announcement to read, which I will read at this time. Senator Robert Francis Kennedy died at 1:44 A.M. today, June 6, 1968." He went on to tell who was at the bedside, omitting several people to shorten his ordeal. Then he added, "He was forty-two years old." Mankiewicz, enfolded in the arms of his friends, wept.

Outside, Mankiewicz makes the announcement
that Robert Kennedy is dying.

120

Campaign staff (Assistant Press Secretory Hugh
McDonald in white shirt) after the announcement.

President Johnson sends Air Force One to bring RFK's body back to New York.

The family is silhouetted against the plane's side by TV lights.

Win or Lose, He Would Have Made a Difference

Bobby Kennedy died just under twenty-six hours after the shooting at the Ambassador Hotel. In a sense, it was appropriate that this tough yet gentle man, whose adult life had developed in turbulence, was cut down in public, within earshot of a roaring crowd, yet died in the setting most typical of his private life, with family and with friends.

While he was alive, the Bobby Kennedy for whom close friends would gladly have given their lives, whom children and blacks and Hispanics loved, never quite filtered through to much of the population, who saw him as arrogant and opportunistic. Only in death, when he was no longer pushing and battling impatiently, did he come through to a greater segment of Americans. For much of the anti-Bobby passion was rooted more in fear of what he might do than in anything he actually did. After June 6, 1968, there no longer was anything he could do.

For eleven weeks he had campaigned for the presidency virtually unprotected, tugged and pulled by swarms of people. Most in the frenzied crowds loved him, but always there were some who hated him. There were wild-eyed bearded hippies in San Francisco shouting "Fascist pig" at him. There were right-wing fanatics, and black-power militants to whom Kennedy was part of the hated white establishment. There were various fringe radicals carrying signs demanding "Open the Archives" and asking "Who Killed Your Brother?" — as if anyone could care more about that subject than Bobby did.

In small towns and large, Robert Kennedy had stood on street corners or in town squares as thousands milled about.

Bobby, Jr., Jacqueline Kennedy, and other family members and friends escort the casket from the plane at LaGuardia Airport, New York.

Often there were young men on rooftops — could one of them be armed? Kennedy was against the Vietnam War, which to some made him a traitor, but he opposed unilateral withdrawal, which to others made him a murderer. He had taken a strong stand on every vital issue of his time, including Israel's right to exist, which Sirhan Sirhan, for one, could not abide. That this issue cost him his life is a matter of some importance, but not a great deal. If not that issue, it could have been some other.

Often, during his whirlwind campaign, Bobby Kennedy would be found alone with his dog, Freckles, or perhaps with a friend. Much to their amazement, people sometimes found themselves encountering the famous figure in a hotel elevator or on a stairway with no security around. When his staff or reporters admonished him for taking such risks, his response was always a variation of "If anyone wants to kill me, it won't be difficult." After he was gone, all those close to him realized that they could have made it more difficult.

Flying back to Washington late one night on his chartered plane, Kennedy had sipped his usual bourbon on the rocks as three newsmen badgered him about security. Dick Harwood of the *Washington Post* asked if he would at least give up the open car if he was elected. "No," said Kennedy, as if he had already given the matter some thought. "We can't have that kind of country — where the president of the United States is afraid to go among the people. I won't ride around in an armored car." Thereafter, in his campaign speeches, he seemed to emphasize the point by assuring his audiences that he wanted to "bring the presidency back to the people." He would visit them, he would walk among them, if he was elected. In saying this, Kennedy no doubt had the White House–bound President Johnson more in mind than JFK, assassinated in an open car in Dallas.

A formal police salute meets the funeral train,
twenty-one cars long, along the tracks at Trenton, New Jersey.

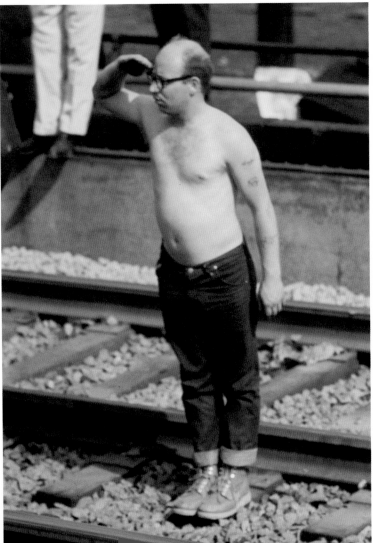

From the day he declared his candidacy until the day he died, the newsmen and newswomen regularly assigned to him rarely skipped a single one of his appearances. They covered him as no candidate has been covered before or probably since. They rarely said why, but Kennedy and his staff understood. The memory of John Kennedy's death was too fresh. No one dared be far away lest the same thing should happen to Bobby.

Gazing up from the floor the night of his shooting, Robert Kennedy, still lucid, wore a haunting expression that no one who knew him and saw it will ever forget. Bobby Kennedy was fully aware of what had happened. He didn't look befuddled. His eyes didn't ask ''what happened?'' He was in pain, and it was clearly mapped on his face. From just a few feet away, I was struck first by horror, and then by the heartbreaking realization that Bobby's time had come and that he knew it.

Of course, his name was Kennedy, but there must have been something more than the name. Thousands of people came to pay their respects at the funeral mass in St. Patrick's Cathedral in New York, and more stood along the train route to Washington. There was little on the exterior of the funeral train to distinguish it other than the black crepe draped on the locomotive and on the observation car. Yet the train had a unique and tragic mission: to carry Robert F. Kennedy toward his final place of rest in Arlington National Cemetery in Virginia, just a few yards from where John F. Kennedy lay buried.

No one will ever know how many Americans turned out along the route of the funeral train. It could have been millions. They waved, and many of them wept. Some held up crudely drawn signs: "Good-bye, Bobby," "Bobby — We'll

People express sorrow in their own way.

Miss You." One little group of people were in rowboats half a mile or so away. They stood up unsteadily and waved at the slow-moving train. Alongside the tracks, at irregular intervals, people sang "The Battle Hymn of the Republic," their impromptu voices rising with the chorus of "Glory, glory hallelujah." During much of the trip, Ethel, who was visited one or two at a time by mourning friends, remained in the observation car, her head frequently resting against her husband's casket. She looked up and smiled when she heard the singing, even though the singers couldn't see her. She loved people to love Bobby. When the crowds disappeared, as the train chugged through barren or inaccessible terrain, she would lower her head again.

So many people were on the train that it soon became clear to Ethel that the visitations to the observation car would not accommodate everyone she wanted to greet. So, to universal astonishment, she appeared at the rear of a passenger coach, offered a smile and a greeting — occasionally a quip — to absolutely everyone, then walked on through the remaining cars, repeating her display of warmth and appreciation. After her brave walk-through no one dared to be too somber. When it was over Ethel retreated to the observation car and to Bobby; her children, her husband's sisters, and three close friends stood vigil with her.

Another Kennedy widow aboard the train did not try to emulate Ethel. Jackie Kennedy remained confined with relatives and close friends in a small roomette in the family car. Who can say what her thoughts were as she endured this experience yet again?

Five hours and forty minutes behind schedule, the procession left Washington's Union Station and made its way past enormous crowds to the burial site. A final irony that Bobby Kennedy would have enjoyed: a special bus carrying the press that had covered the entire campaign was accorded a place not far behind the hearse. Immediately behind that bus was the limousine bearing an outraged president of the United States, Bobby Kennedy's old nemesis, Lyndon Baines Johnson. Another limousine, following the president's, bore the vice president, Hubert Humphrey. Johnson could not abide the notion that a bunch of reporters and photographers had been given precedence over the president and the vice president. When a Secret Service agent dispatched by Johnson boarded the bus and ordered the driver to allow the two limousines to move ahead of it, the agent was greeted by a torrent of jeers so menacing that he hopped off, and the bus remained in place. More fearful of Johnsonian wrath than of the journalists' Bronx cheers, the agent reboarded and again ordered the driver to let the two limousines pass. Dick Tuck, usually a joker but deadly serious this time, ordered the hapless Secret Service "spook" off the bus. The agent left, but he returned momentarily. The justifiably nervous driver moved the bus over a lane, and the presidential and vice presidential cars zoomed ahead. It was an incident that Bobby Kennedy would have relished.

The white headstones at Arlington came into view. Prayers were said, candles flickered in the darkness, tears were shed. Friends, bonded by shared experience and now-shattered expectations, would wonder then — and through the 1968 campaign of Humphrey and Nixon, and all through the decades to come — what turns history would have taken if only Bobby Kennedy had lived. As a world leader and peacemaker, or as the intensely driven seeker of a more just nation — president or not — he would have made a difference.

Mourners greeted the train across its 226-mile journey. In Wilmington,
a Delaware State Trooper salutes.

ACKNOWLEDGMENTS

In 1989, Joe Traver, photojournalist and Regional Director of the National Press Photographers Association, Buffalo, approached Bill Eppridge with the idea of pulling together a slide show on Robert F. Kennedy's 1968 presidential campaign for a regional meeting of the NPPA. Traver was familiar with Eppridge's famous images of RFK from the days of the original *Life* magazine, and thought people would appreciate seeing unpublished photographs from that period.

Much of Eppridge's other work had perished in a 1974 Los Angeles canyon fire, which also destroyed his home. At the time of the fire, he had started working on a book of his photographs from the 1960s that would have included many of the pictures from RFK's campaign. He wasn't sure then how much of his work from that era still existed, and he was reluctant to dredge up painful memories.

Responding to Traver's persistence, Eppridge finally agreed to go back into the *Life* magazine picture files, where he discovered that his work had been meticulously preserved by the staffs of both the Time Inc. Picture Collection and the Time-Life Photo Lab. From these archives he assembled the slide lecture that ultimately led to this book.

With the twenty-fifth anniversary of the tragic assassination approaching, Eppridge teamed with friend and collaborator Hays Gorey, who had covered the campaign for *Time*. The result is *Robert Kennedy: The Last Campaign*.

The authors are indebted to the following, without whose help and support the project would have been impossible to complete:

Adrienne Aurichio, Alicia Aurichio, Bob Buckley and his photo lab crew, Bobbi Baker Burrows, Russell Burrows, Dick Pollard, Philip Kunhardt, Roy Rowan, George P. Hunt, Ralph Graves, Richard B. Stolley, Bernard Quint, John Downey, Hans Kohl, Rob Richie, Mary Domster, Ann Wyman, Jimmy Wilson, Stu Ruby, Charles Quinn, Loudon Wainwright, Robert F. Jones, Louise Jones, Margaret Ferguson, Jay Eyerman, John Frook, Norma Frook, Carmine Ercolano, George Karas, Sylvia Wright, Clif and Vi Edom, Jane Glenn, Gordon Parks, Carl Mydans, Alfred Eisenstadt, the technicians in the Time-Life Photo Lab, Mel Levine, Mike Miller, Steve Fine, Dot McMahon, Bill Luster, our editors, Pat Strachan and Joy Press, Sarah Lazin, Ronald L. Goldfarb, Laura Nolan, David Friend, Mary Jane McGonegal, Maryann Kornely, Beth Zarcone, Mary Doherty, Lucky Beckett, Holly Holden, Rich Clarkson, Heinz Kluetmeier, Richard LoPinto of Nikon, Bill Pakala, Sam Garcia and Ron Taniwaki of Nikon Professional Services, Doris O'Neill, Lydia D'moch, Heike Hinch, Lutgardo Rodriguez, David Hough, Frank Curtis, Warren Wallerstein, Vaughn Andrews, Chrissie Wolford, the staff of *Life* magazine during 1966 and 1968, Frank Mankiewicz, Melody Miller, Jerry Ter Horst, Fred Dutton, and special thanks to Joe Traver.

Bill Eppridge and Hays Gorey, February 1993